STILLING THE MIND

Düdjom Lingpa (1835–1904)

Drawing by Winfield Klein

Stilling the Mind

SHAMATHA TEACHINGS
FROM DÜDJOM LINGPA'S
VAJRA ESSENCE

B. Alan Wallace
Edited by Brian Hodel

Wisdom Publications
199 Elm Street
Somerville MA 02144 USA
wisdompubs.org

Library of Congress Cataloging-in-Publication Data
Wallace, B. Alan.
  Stilling the mind : shamatha teachings from Dudjom Lingpa's Vajra
essense / B. Alan Wallace ; edited by Brian Hodel.
    p. cm.
  Includes bibliographical references and index.
  ISBN 0-86171-690-6 (alk. paper)
  1. Śamatha (Buddhism) 2. Attention—Religious aspects—Buddhism. I.
Hodel, Brian. II. Title.
  BQ7805.W355 2011
  294.3'4435—dc23

                                    2011022674

ISBN 978-0-86171-690-6
eBook ISBN 978-0-86171-649-4

21 20 19 18
6 5   4   3

Cover design by Phil Pascuzzo. Drawing by Winfield Klein.
Interior design by LC. Set in Weiss 11/15.

Wisdom Publications' books are printed on acid-free paper and meet the
guidelines for permanence and durability of the Production Guidelines for
Book Longevity of the Council on Library Resources.

♲.This book was produced with environmental mindfulness.
For more information, please visit wisdompubs.org/wisdom-environment.

Printed in the United States of America.

Please visit fscus.org.

CONTENTS

PREFACE

S tudents of Tibetan Buddhism in the West have been extremely fortunate in recent decades to receive teachings from great lamas who were trained in Tibet before the Chinese Communist occupation. These superb teachers include the Dalai Lama, the Sixteenth Karmapa, Düdjom Rinpoche, Sakya Trizin Rinpoche, and many other great masters. There has also been a gradual increase in the number of texts from this tradition available in Western languages, as more and more students have learned the art of translation. As a result, we are now seeing a significant number of Westerners who have themselves become qualified teachers of Tibetan Buddhism, as well as a younger generation of Tibetan lamas who were educated in India and other regions of the Tibetan diaspora.

Despite these exceptionally favorable circumstances, it remains difficult for us to properly contextualize the teachings we receive and to put them into practice effectively. Tibetan teachers, as wise, experienced, and enthusiastic as they often are, and Western students—many of them willing to make great sacrifices to practice Dharma—are still, culturally speaking, worlds apart. Keep in mind that Tibetan Buddhism began its development in the eighth century and is itself an offshoot of Indian Buddhism, which began with Shakyamuni Buddha around 500 B.C.E. The distinctive qualities of these traditional Asian cultures are quite different from those of the modern world in which we live today. It took roughly four hundred years for Indian Buddhism to morph into Tibetan Buddhism.

Now the infusion of Tibetan Buddhism into today's global setting—the first globalization of Buddhism in its entire 2,500-year history—is taking place at a breathtaking pace.

The Buddhist texts and commentaries presented to people today were initially geared for the lives, and especially the *psyches*, of ancient, Asian students of Dharma. The cultural context of a second-century Indian or even a nineteenth-century Tibetan has very little in common with our globalized world of jet planes, cell phones, and the internet. Certainly we can gain a great deal from reading such timeless classics as Shantideva's *Guide to the Bodhisattva Way of Life* or Patrül Rinpoche's *Words of My Perfect Teacher*. Great human and universal truths are expressed there that apply to all human cultures. At the level of particulars, however, Shantideva and Patrül Rinpoche were speaking primarily to students with views, values, and lifestyles radically different from ours.

Therefore, as a Western teacher of Dharma who has had the great good fortune, over more than forty years, to study with a number of eminent Tibetan Buddhist teachers, I have tried to mold my commentary on the *Vajra Essence* to the Western psyche. That, after all, is what I myself had to do in order to gain some understanding of Tibetan Buddhism. I have addressed a number of issues that often cause confusion among Western students, ranging from terminology (with terms sometimes defined differently in the context of different traditions and teachings), to the significance of specific techniques within important sequences of meditation practices. It is my hope that as a Westerner with much in common with other Western Buddhists, I will be able to provide a bridge between worlds. I am, after all, someone who grew up mostly in southern California, went to high school, dreamed of becoming a wildlife biologist, played the piano, and—after being a monk for fourteen years—reentered Western society pursuing interests in both science and religion. I am fluent in Tibetan but am also fascinated by quantum cosmology, the cognitive sciences, and the wonders of modern technology.

The text presented here, the *Vajra Essence* by Düdjom Lingpa, a nineteenth-century master of the Nyingma order of Tibetan Buddhism, is known as the *Nelug Rangjung* in Tibetan, meaning "the natural emergence of the nature of existence."¹ This is an ideal teaching in which to unravel some of the common misunderstandings of Tibetan Buddhism, since it is a sweeping practice that can take one from the basics all the way to enlightenment in a single lifetime. The present volume explains the initial section on *shamatha*, or meditative quiescence, about nine percent of the entire *Vajra Essence* root text.

Shamatha is presented in the *Vajra Essence* as a foundational practice on the Dzogchen path. Dzogchen, often translated as "the Great Perfection," is the highest of the nine vehicles (*yanas*) in the Nyingma tradition of Tibetan Buddhism. Classically speaking, after achieving shamatha, the yogi will use his or her newly acquired powers of concentration to practice insight into the nature of emptiness (*vipashyana*), followed by the Dzogchen practices of *tregchö* (breakthrough) and *tögal* (direct crossing-over). These four practices comprise the essential path to enlightenment from the Nyingma point of view. The practice of Dzogchen brings one into direct contact with reality, unmediated by the individual personality or society.

Shamatha, in its various presentations, is used to make the mind pliant and serviceable for the more advanced practices. Shamatha is not found only in Buddhism. This practice of refining attention skills exists in religious contexts as distinct as Hinduism, Taoism, early Christianity, and the Sufi schools of Islam. Within Tibetan Buddhism, shamatha practice maps on to the nine stages of attentional development wherein thoughts gradually subside as concentrative power is increased to the point at which one can effortlessly maintain single-pointed focus on a chosen object for at least four hours. The accomplishment of shamatha is accompanied by a powerful experience of bliss, luminosity, and stillness.

Shamatha requires more careful incubation than most other kinds of meditation. You can practice *tonglen* (taking on the suffering of others and giving them your happiness) very well while you are watching the news. Loving-kindness and compassion and the rest of the four immeasurables can be practiced down on "Main Street." Vipashyana you can cultivate anywhere. In fact, many other practices can be done under varying circumstances. If you wish to take shamatha all the way to its ground, however, it requires a supportive, serene environment, good diet, proper exercise, and very few preoccupations. The necessary internal conditions are minimal desires, few activities and concerns, contentment, pure ethical discipline, and freedom from obsessive, compulsive thinking. It is my feeling that the achievement of shamatha is so rare today because those circumstances are so rare. It is difficult to find a conducive environment in which to practice at length and without interference—even more so to have that and access to suitable spiritual friends for support and guidance. Therefore, if the causes are difficult to bring together, the result—shamatha—is also necessarily rare. I present a detailed guide to the general practice of shamatha in my earlier book, *The Attention Revolution* (Wisdom, 2006).

Düdjom Lingpa was a lay practitioner, married, and the father of eight renowned sons, including Jigmé Tenpai Nyima, the Third Dodrupchen Rinpoche, who was widely revered by lamas of all the Tibetan Buddhist orders. During the course of his life, Düdjom Lingpa performed many miracles, and he reached the highest levels of realization of tantra as well as the Great Perfection. Thirteen of his disciples attained the rainbow body—dissolution into light at death—and one thousand became *vidyadhara* tantric masters through gaining insight into the essential nature of awareness. In short, he was one of the most realized and acclaimed Tibetan lamas of his time.

The *Vajra Essence* was essentially "downloaded" from the dharmakaya, the buddha mind that is essentially coterminous with the ultimate ground of reality, and brought into our world in 1862, when Düdjom Lingpa was twenty-seven years old. He received it in a vision as a mind *terma*.[2] However, while it was optimal for him to receive it in 1862, only about thirteen years later did the time come for it to be made public. It is clear from the opening that this text is not scholastic in nature but is intended for those who are dedicated to practice.

In the initial section on shamatha, the *Vajra Essence* has the practitioner take the mind as the path, using the specific approach of *taking appearances and awareness as the path*, also known as *settling the mind in its natural state*. In brief, this consists of observing all arising mental phenomena without grasping on to them. Your thoughts, emotions, images, and so forth are observed closely with mindfulness, but you do not encourage, discourage, or involve yourself in any way with the arising mental phenomena. The aim at this stage is to settle the mind in the substrate consciousness (*alayavijñana*)—the ground of the ordinary mind. The text also comments on the many meditation experiences (*nyam*) that may be encountered and how to behave when they appear. Pitfalls are described, along with some of the deeper possibilities of this phase of practice.

One of the central themes of the opening section of the *Vajra Essence* is how crucial shamatha is for success with more advanced practices, such as meditation on emptiness, tantric generation and completion practices, and Dzogchen. Given that the Buddha himself strongly emphasized the importance of developing shamatha and uniting it with vipashyana, it is remarkable the degree to which this key foundational practice is marginalized or overlooked entirely in all schools of Buddhism today. It seems that nearly everyone is in a mad rush to ascend to more advanced forms of meditation without noticing that the mind they are depending on for this is heavily prone to alternating laxity and excitation. In traditional Buddhist texts, such an attentionally imbalanced mind is considered dysfunctional, and it is unreasonable to think that such a mind can effectively enter into meditations designed to sever mental afflictions at their roots. Although you can practice more advanced meditations without first achieving shamatha, you are bound to hit a plateau and then stagnate in your practice without recognizing that it is failing due to insufficient preparation in first refining attention.

Düdjom Lingpa's treatise explains a number of integrated practices, giving me the opportunity to provide some detailed comparisons among meditation techniques and their aims—something that can be easily missed by those unable to remain in intimate contact over long periods with their teachers. Such logistical problems, common to Westerners who must maintain careers and relationships while studying and practicing Dharma, often result in a lack of full understanding of the relationships among a wide variety of elements of Dharma. The difference in language and cultural background between teacher and student only exacerbates this problem. Here I have tried to use my own experience to fill in some of these gaps.

My commentary returns again and again to one particular dilemma presented in this initial section of the *Vajra Essence*: In its descriptions of meditation states, does the language at a given point refer to the substrate consciousness—the *alayavijñana*—or to the dharmakaya—that is, pristine awareness, or *rigpa*? The substrate consciousness is the foundation and source of an individual's psyche. Accessing it is the proper end of shamatha practice. The dharmakaya, or buddha mind, on the other hand, is much deeper than the individual mind, and that is realized through the practice of Dzogchen. The answer to the question of which "ground" of consciousness is indicated in a given passage depends both on the context in which similar terms are presented and in the nature of the experiences described. It is extremely important that this distinction be clearly understood, because it points to a major misunderstanding to which the uninformed practitioner can easily fall prey. So the question—"Is he talking about the substrate consciousness or the dharmakaya?"—runs like a thread throughout the commentary.

I address a number of such specific pitfalls pointed out in the root text, along with obscure and sometimes controversial issues such as the *siddhis*, or paranormal abilities, we obtain as we advance along the path. These include clairvoyance and walking through walls, powers that most Westerners—with their scientific and often secular upbringing—may find incredible. How are we to take these? Are they metaphor, myth, or reality? There are many complex issues in fully translating a document such as this, which is esoteric and subtle even for Tibetans, into a vernacular that can be absorbed by a contemporary audience that did not grow up steeped in this tradition.

One crucial area to examine at the outset of any study of Buddhist texts is the motivation that animates our efforts. There are many motivations for entering the Dharma. One example that I think is quite prevalent, especially in the West, is using Dharma to make samsara, or cyclic existence, more comfortable. Such a motivation is quite understandable—life has a lot of sharp edges. Today there is fear of terrorism, and as always we experience illness, conflict between spouses, unhappiness at losing a job—tension, depression, anxiety. Therefore, many people practice Dharma in order to cope better with modern living and feel a bit more comfortable. There's nothing wrong with that. But if the Dharma is reduced entirely to a kind of therapy, its essence is lost. The *Vajra Essence* is a teaching that can enable you to achieve enlightenment in one lifetime. It has done so for many practitioners. So its value goes far beyond smoothing samsara's rough spots. The true value of the Dharma is as a vehicle to the enlightened state in order to be of greatest benefit in the world.

To fully benefit from the teachings here, it is best to honor the fundamental teachings common to all schools of Buddhism; do not, in other words, indulge the feeling that you are somehow superior to the most basic teachings—the four noble truths, the four applications of mindfulness, the four immeasurables, and so forth. Not a single syllable spoken by the Buddha is too basic. All the words of the Buddha have a single taste and can be put into practice as means to liberation. It is best as well to revere the Mahayana, not thinking of the approach requiring three countless eons treading the path to enlightenment—the cultivation of the six perfections, the insights presented in the Yogachara and the Madhyamaka views, and so on—as being beneath you. Though you may practice Dzogchen, the highest vehicle, you should not look down on Yogachara or Madhyamaka teachings. Finally, an ideal vessel for these teachings values the tantras of all three classes—outer, inner, and secret—and has a genuine desire to practice *tregchö* and *tögal*, the two stages of Dzogchen. In other words, such a student yearns to really put these into practice in this lifetime.

Another commonly held mistaken attitude toward Dharma is the thought, "Oh, but that's too high for me. I should always just stick with the basics." It doesn't take much experience of trying to settle the mind to conclude that one is just not cut out for enlightenment and that one should just ramp down one's expectations, leaving the exalted states for those who are more gifted. But this would be a mistake. Don't think that Dzogchen is beyond your reach. It takes courage to believe that such teachings are within your reach, but actually they were designed for people like us. You can do it.

THE EVOLUTION OF THIS BOOK

The *Vajra Essence* is one of the great jewels of Dharma—unified in its adherence to the central truth of pervasive enlightened reality, while reflecting a brilliant array of interpenetrating teachings and realizations. It has been my heartfelt intention, in both the translation and commentary, to make this great teaching clear and accessible to modern students of Dharma. If this volume is true to the original intent of Düdjom Lingpa and at the same time completely contemporary in its presentation, then I will have achieved my aspiration.

The *Vajra Essence* has special relevance for us today in the West: In one of Düdjom Lingpa's dreams, a *devaputra*, a celestial being named Dungi Zurphu, prophesied that the benefit from his profound hidden treasures, his *termas*, would go west, saying, "Those deserving to be tamed by you dwell in human cities to the west." With the wish to help fulfill that prophecy, the present translation of his hidden treasure the *Vajra Essence* was made under the guidance of the Venerable Gyatrul Rinpoche, who has been teaching in the West since 1972. Gyatrul Rinpoche received the oral transmission of this text three times from three of the emanations of Düdjom Lingpa: In Tibet he received it from Jamyang Natsog Rangdröl and from Tulku Künzang Nyima, and later in Nepal he received it from His Holiness Düdjom Rinpoche Jigdral Yeshe Dorje, the Supreme Head of the Nyingma order of Tibetan Buddhism.

Intermittently from the autumn of 1995 to the summer of 1998, I read through this text twice with Gyatrul Rinpoche, receiving many points of clarification from him. While working on a first-draft translation, he went through the text line by line with a small group of his disciples including myself, carefully correcting errors in my translation and elucidating points of lingering uncertainty in my own comprehension of the text. Most of the annotations throughout the translation are based upon his oral commentary.

The excerpt presented in this volume, where it is integrated with my commentary, is virtually identical to that contained in a new complete translation published by Vimala Publications, the publishing arm of Gyatrul Rinpoche's organization. Access to the *Vajra Essence* is traditionally reserved only for those who have had the proper initiations and permissions from their teachers, and its secrecy has been carefully preserved by the lineage. However, the shamatha section in this volume and the succeeding section on vipashyana in a later volume are not considered restricted material, and their publication for the general public here has been authorized by Gyatrul Rinpoche.

The evolution of my commentary began when I finished translating the *Vajra Essence*, at which point Gyatrul Rinpoche authorized me to teach the entire text. I felt that I had never encountered a more precious treatise setting out the entire path to enlightenment, so I took his words deeply to heart, wishing to share this mind treasure in the most meaningful way I could. I have found that the practice of Vajrayana Buddhism, including the Great Perfection, is inadequate without a firm theoretical and experiential foundation in the more fundamental teachings of Buddhism. By overlooking the core teachings and practices of shamatha and vipashyana meditation and the altruistic mind of bodhichitta, or the spirit of awakening, the insights and resulting transformations from these practices are not realized. And due to overlooking this foundation, the practice of Vajrayana by itself fails to yield authentic Vajrayana realizations.

I decided therefore to teach a series of retreats to a few experienced Dharma students focusing in sequence on shamatha, the four close applications of mindfulness, the four immeasurables, the Madhyamaka approach to vipashyana practice, including dream yoga, and finally an introduction to the Great Perfection. After I had taught this entire series of week-long retreats over the course of two years, I led four more week-long retreats on selected sections of the *Vajra Essence* focusing on shamatha, vipashyana, *tregchö*, and *tögal*. One of my students offered to transcribe my oral commentaries on these extended passages from the text. I shared these transcripts with other students, who reported they found them very helpful and inspiring. It then occurred to me to make the first two of these commentaries, edited, available in book form, so I asked Gyatrul Rinpoche whether he would allow me to publish for the general public my commentaries on just the shamatha and vipashyana sections of the *Vajra Essence*. He agreed, and with the help of those mentioned below, the first of these two commentaries is now a reality.

ACKNOWLEDGMENTS

I am deeply grateful to Venerable Gyatrul Rinpoche for opening this treasure to us for the benefit of all those who may read our translation. I am also indebted to Dr. Yeshi Dhonden, Khenpo Tsewang Gyatso, and Tulku Pema Wangyal for elucidating some points of the text, and to Sangye Khandro for reading through the entire manuscript and making many helpful suggestions.

I would like to express my thanks to the following students of Gyatrul Rinpoche for their invaluable comments and corrections in preparing the translation. They include Deborah Borin, Ana Carreon, Les Collins, Scott Globus, Steve Goodman, Mimi Hohenberg, Willie Korman, Naomi Mattis, and Lindy Steele. My thanks go also to Elissa Mannheimer, who line edited the entire translation. After she was finished, I carefully read through the edited translation twice again, making many further corrections and changes, so any lingering errors in the translation are solely my responsibility; and I hope that scholars and contemplatives more knowledgeable than I will bring them to my notice.

For his invaluable work on this commentary, special thanks go to Wisdom Publications' senior editor David Kittelstrom and line editor Lea Groth-Wilson, along with Carol Levy, who transcribed my oral commentary, Dion Blundell, editor of the new Vimala edition of the root text, and Brian Hodel, who prepared the original draft of this volume and guided it through its editorial development.

1

INTRODUCTION

Unlike the vast majority of Tibetan texts, the *Vajra Essence* is not sub-divided into sections and subsections. It is written instead as a stream of consciousness that flows unimpededly for some four hundred pages. My translation, however, does divide it into chapters with subsections in order to help the reader navigate the material.

We begin with the introduction, which in many Dharma texts has two parts. First comes the homage, and second is the author's promise to compose the text, to take it to its completion. This text is no exception to that rule, although of course in this case the author didn't so much "compose" the text as he simply manifested it—an act very much in the spirit of Dzogchen.

> Homage to the manifest face of Samantabhadra himself,
> the Omnipresent Lord, the original, primordial ground!

> The enlightened awareness lineage of the buddhas is so desig-
> nated because the minds of all the buddhas of the three times are
> of one taste in the absolute space of phenomena. The symbolic
> lineage of the vidyadharas is so designated because the symbolic
> signs of ultimate reality, the treasury of space, spontaneously
> emerge, without reliance upon the stages of spiritual training and
> practice. The aural lineage of ordinary individuals is so designated

because these practical instructions naturally arise in verbal transmission as an entrance to the disciples' paths, like filling a vase.

The homage—to Samantabhadra, the Primordial Buddha, the Timeless Buddha, the Buddha from which all other buddhas manifest—is quite concise. That is followed by a reference to the three lineages of the Dzogchen tradition, the first of which I am translating as "the enlightened awareness lineage of the buddhas." This lineage is identified thus because the minds of the buddhas are indistinguishable and of the same nature. This being so, there is no transmission as such.

This initial paragraph introduces some crucial terms, which I will provide in Sanskrit, since they are given different translations into English. The "absolute space of phenomena" is my translation for *dharmadhatu*. *Dharma* in this context means "phenomena." *Dhatu* means "domain," "element," "space," or "realm." "Absolute space" here means the space out of which relative space, time, mind, matter, and all other dualities and all other phenomena emerge. It is the ground of being, the primordial ground. Its relationship with primordial consciousness (*jñana*) is nondual.

Primordial consciousness, your own *rigpa*, or pristine awareness, is that out of which all relative states of consciousness emerge and is nondual from the absolute space of phenomena. In that ultimate reality, the minds of all the buddhas—past, present, and future—are all of the same taste in that absolute space of phenomena. They are undifferentiated. This, then, is the ultimate lineage—if indeed we can label something that transcends time and is inconceivable as a "lineage."

The second of these three Dzogchen lineages is the "symbolic lineage of the vidyadharas." *Vidya* is Sanskrit for *rigpa*, "pristine awareness"; *dhara* is "one who holds." So a *vidyadhara* is literally "one who holds pristine awareness." A more precise meaning is "one who has gained a conceptually unmediated, nondual realization of rigpa, of buddha nature." This is a lineage transmitted from vidyadhara to vidyadhara. It is not vidyadhara to ordinary sentient being, nor vidyadhara to buddha, but rather a community of vidyadharas, similar to the classic meaning of *sangha*, comprised exclusively of *aryas*—those who have gained a nonconceptual, unmediated realization of emptiness. In this case it is a sangha of vidyadharas, and they have a way of communicating, of transmitting Dharma horizontally—not down to us, not up to the buddhas. Their method is symbolic, and as such, it is not verbal in the ordinary sense of the term.

"The symbolic lineage of the vidyadharas is so designated because the symbolic signs of ultimate reality..." Here is another crucial term. In Sanskrit, "ultimate reality" is *dharmata*. *Dharma*, again, means "phenomena"; *ta* is like "ness," making for "dharma-ness," or "phenomena-ness," an abstract noun. This refers to the very nature of being dharmas, of being phenomena. *Dharmata* is a synonym for emptiness, for "thatness," and for "suchness": just that—reality itself.

The "symbolic signs," the symbolic manifestations, the archetypal symbols "of ultimate reality, the treasury of space"—this last term is used interchangeably with ultimate reality, space being of course empty, and a treasury—"spontaneously emerge," they just appear, like bubbles rising in water, "without reliance upon the stages of spiritual training and practice." In other words, this is pure discovery. They appear spontaneously. This is not the result of striving diligently along the path of training or practice— a developmental approach. Until we become vidyadharas, we needn't be too concerned with this. Basically we are being told that vidyadharas have a way of symbolically communicating with each other.

The third lineage is the one most pertinent to us: the "aural lineage of ordinary individuals"—folks like us. Note that it is not *verbal* but *aural*. In Tibetan, aural lineage is *nyengyü*. *Nyen* means "to listen," as in something is coming to the ears. How do we receive the transmission of Dzogchen? Through the aural lineage of ordinary individuals. It is "so designated because these practical instructions..."—the Tibetan word means teachings that are synthesized into practice from the vast body of Buddhist teachings—"naturally arise in verbal transmission," in words, "as an entrance to the disciples' paths, like filling a vase."

The practical instructions tell you what you actually need to do as opposed to receiving and assimilating a mass of theoretical context, background, and the like. The words being transmitted from mouth to ear—filling your heart and mind, like filling a vase with ambrosia, opening the way to your own path to enlightenment—are the entrance, the gateway.

So, depending on context, the transmission of Dzogchen can be mind to mind, it can be symbolic, or it can be verbal.

DÜDJOM LINGPA AND THE *VAJRA ESSENCE*

These instructions were revealed by themselves, not by human beings, as the magical display of primordial consciousness. May I, the spiritual mentor of the world, embodying these three lineages, being blessed with the inexhaustible ornamental wheels of the three secrets of the buddhas and bodhisattvas, and holding the permission of the Three Roots and the oceanic, oath-bound guardians, bring this to perfection.

What is the source of these teachings? The ultimate source, the ground of the teachings, is not some human being. They arise spontaneously from the dharmata—the teacher is the Buddha. At this point we must take care, because the presentations and commentaries of teachings such as these are made by human teachers. They are not infallible. No matter how high the realization of the teacher, our task as students is not simply to absorb the words of the teaching and then apply them unquestioningly like soldiers acting under orders. In Buddhism we often encounter the metaphor of the empty vessel that is appropriate to be filled by the teachings, and we may come to believe that all the wisdom is coming from the teacher's side and that we as students must absorb it uncritically.

Though the teacher should not blindly be viewed as literally infallible, nevertheless every word is there to arouse our intelligence, to awaken our heart, to draw forth our buddha nature. As His Holiness the Dalai Lama has so often commented vis-à-vis the Buddhadharma as a whole, one of the core elements of spiritual maturation, which is absolutely antifundamentalist, is developing our own discerning wisdom, our own discerning intelligence. If we ignore such advice, we run the risk of being unable to determine which meanings are definitive and which are interpretive. That can lead us, for instance, to accentuate ultimate reality while completely ignoring conventional reality. We are warned by Padmasambhava and by all of the realized teachers that this is a big mistake. There are two truths for a buddha—the ultimate and the conventional. Neither one stifles the other. They are of one taste.

"May I, the spiritual mentor of the world..." Here the author, Düdjom Lingpa, is using the true referent of the word *I*; he is not referring to some nineteenth-century Tibetan. He knows that he is a vidyadhara. He says so with no pretense, no arrogance; he is just giving us the truth. He tells us he embodies the three aforementioned lineages and that he is "blessed with the inexhaustible ornamental wheels of the three secrets of the buddhas and bodhisattvas." "Ornamental wheels" is a quite literal translation. Gyatrul Rinpoche comments: "The attributes of the buddhas and bodhisattvas are inexhaustible ornaments of reality, which continue on forever like ever-revolving wheels. Hence they are called *inexhaustible ornamental wheels.*" The *three secrets* are the three mysteries—body, speech, and mind. Each contains an element of mystery. What is the true nature of the body of a buddha, the speech of a buddha, the mind of a buddha? That's very deep. The Three Roots are the lama (or spiritual mentor), your *yidam* (or personal deity—Tara, Padmasambhava, Manjushri, or whomever it may be), and the *dakini* (the enlightened feminine principle).

Düdjom Lingpa tells us he has been fully authorized to reveal, to manifest this text. He has been blessed by the qualities of the Buddha. He holds the permission of the Three Roots and the "oceanic, oath-bound guardians." By the blessings of all of these, "May I...bring this to perfection." He doesn't say "compose," but rather he will bring it to perfection, manifest it perfectly. And he does this with the permission of the Three Roots—lama, yidam, and dakini—and the oceanic, oath-bound guardians. These are the *dharmapalas*, the Dharma protectors who have sworn an oath to guard and preserve the Dharma. Therefore, Düdjom Lingpa has a great deal of support for manifesting this text, support that forms part of his commitment to offer it: May I bring this to perfection; may I reveal it perfectly.

The primordial, originally pure nature of existence, which is great, intellect-transcending, ultimate reality, free of conceptual elaboration, is obscured by conceiving of a self and grasping at duality. Because of this, individuals are bound by clinging to the true existence of the three delusive realms of samsara.[3] Still, there are those who have accumulated vast merit over many eons and who have the power of pure aspirations. Therefore, for the sake of those with the fortune to master ultimate reality, the treasury of space—by awakening the karmic force of engaging in the action of nonaction in great, self-originating, primordial consciousness—I shall present this fundamental king of tantras, spontaneously arisen from the nature of existence of the sugatagarbha.

"Primordial" is a technical term closely associated with the quality of being "originally pure" (kadag). Ka, being the first syllable of the Tibetan alphabet, implies "primordial," "original," and dag means "pure." However, Gyatrul Rinpoche explains: ka refers to the beginning of time and dag means "pure" in the sense of transcending—in other words, "timeless." So, although "originally pure" is a very common translation for kadag, the term also carries the connotation of transcending time, of being beyond past, present, and future.

Seeking to enrich each statement, this text commonly compounds adjective upon adjective as in "great intellect-transcending" (beyond conceptual grasp), "ultimate reality," (dharmata), and "free of conceptual elaboration." Conceptual elaboration is the entire matrix of "this and that," "up and down"— all of our mental contexts and designations.

Thus, this originally pure nature of existence, this ultimate reality that is free of conceptualization, is obscured by the concept of self, the notion "I am," and by grasping at duality. If "I am," then "you are," and all that other stuff out there "is." Assuming that view, I respond to what's happening to me as if all these phenomena were absolutely real.

We have been given an elegant and very loaded sentence. At this point we could say, "OK, we're finished. That sums up everything." A student who understands the full meaning of this sentence could just go home and practice. But let's probe a little more deeply. Is this sentence no more than an elaborate way of saying that the nature of reality is obscured by thought? You could say that, but that would be only partially correct. Remember that in the practice of tantra and of Dzogchen, all thoughts are regarded as emanations of dharmakaya. Therefore, in those practices, simply putting an end to thoughts would not be appropriate.

Let us focus on something more subtle: *grasping* at thoughts. Here we must use language very carefully because the practice to which we are being introduced is neither elaborate nor complicated; it is very simple. Therefore, the few concepts we use to describe it must be applied with great precision. Otherwise our terms will be confused and all understanding will be lost. What does it mean to grasp at a thought? What is the nature of grasping? The Sanskrit *graha* means "to hold on to," "to grasp." It's exactly that. When you say, "Have you grasped what I was trying to tell you?" this means "Have you understood?" but it also means, have you got a "hold" on it, did you "get" it? And as soon as you have done so, grasping is involved.

We can view a phenomenon such as grasping in gradations from coarse to subtle. The coarsest level of grasping, which blatantly obscures the nature of reality, would be to say something like, "How dare you say that to me! Don't you know who *I am?*" In such a case I, the speaker, am holding on to my great big, thick, robust ego, and since you've infringed upon it, I am reacting aggressively. We can grasp on to possessions as well as personal identity, as in: "This cup isn't mine. Why did you bring me this when *my* cup is in my room?" But grasping needn't be that coarse. When you are asked, "What am I holding in my hand?" and answer, "a cup," you have just grasped on to "cup-ness." You have identified an object within the context of a conceptual framework—a word, a sign. So the mind that latches on to a sign— here an image commonly designated as a "cup"—does so through grasping. Although you are merely identifying "That's a cup," this is also a form of grasping. It may not be the kind of grasping that will lead to endless misery, but it is a subtle form of grasping.

Ultimate reality, then, is obscured by the concept of self. It is not the concept alone that is obscuring ultimate reality. Rather it is the *reification*, the grasping on to the concept, that creates the obscuration. The Tibetan term for reification (*dendzin*) means grasping on to inherent existence, grasping on to true existence. You decontextualize, you grasp something as existing independently, by its own nature. One example is to believe that there really is an inherently existing person—you or me or anyone—that could be praised or insulted. Moreover, anything believed to exist by itself is a product of reification. This reification is the root of samsara, the cycle of existence. On the other hand, grasping is a broader term. When I hold up a cup and ask, "What is this?" your answer that it is a cup doesn't necessarily mean you are grasping on to it as truly existent. It is still grasping in that you are holding on to the concept of "cup-ness," but by designating it as a cup you are not necessarily reifying it by grasping on to it as inherently real. It is possible to use language without being trapped by it, although generally we are unable to avoid it. To sum up, grasping can be more or less subtle, and one form of grasping is reification, the grasping on to inherent existence.

In the proper context grasping can be very useful. Madhyamaka insight practices can employ grasping to deliver you from grasping. Subtle grasping is also used in the tantric stage of generation, which is saturated by grasping. There, visualizing your environment as a pure land and imagining yourself as a deity, you develop some understanding that your normal sense of identity is only a construct, that it is conceptually designated. In those practices you are removing that construct and substituting another identity, one that is much closer to reality than your ordinary one. Seeing all of your thoughts as expressions of *dharmakaya*, all sounds as *sambhogakaya*, and all appearances as *nirmanakaya* is grasping. You are seeing them *as* something, overlaying an interpretation upon them. However, in Vajrayana Buddhism that is very useful grasping.

Bear in mind, though, that from a Buddhist perspective you do not consciously, deliberately use grasping on to true existence—reification—as part of the path. In Vajrayana particularly you avoid that. When you are generating divine pride or pure vision and so forth, you do not think, "I'm really a buddha," or "this is really Padmasambhava," and grasp on to the vision as having inherent existence. The whole point of Vajrayana is to simultaneously maintain the awareness of the emptiness of self, other, the environment, and so forth, together with the divine pride and pure vision. All of that is held in a delicate balance. In the same breath you generate the deity, the divine pride, and pure vision, knowing that all of it is apparitional. Therefore grasping is a tool to be used on the path but reification is not. Grasping also has its uses in Dzogchen. In most cases we cannot simply go directly to utter simplicity; we need teachings and methods to help us arrive there.

Because of this reification of the concept of self, grasping on to duality, "individuals are bound by clinging to the true existence"—a term that means existing by its own nature, independent of conceptual designation—"of the three delusive realms of samsara." "Delusive" is a good translation of the Tibetan *trülpa*. Phenomena, appearances, are not deluded; it is we sentient beings who are deluded about them. For instance, the color of a person's hair is not deluded, but it invites the delusion of sentient beings. Why? Because it appears to us to be truly existent from its own side—some phenomenon way over there that exists independently of my perception of it over here. It appears that I am merely a passive witness of truly existing phenomena, and in that way appearances are delusive or misleading. This delusion binds us to samsara.

In a striking metaphor, one of the most powerful I have seen in all of Buddhism, Tsongkhapa refers to existence in samsara as being in an iron cage, shackled, blind, in a river—a torrent, actually—in the pitch black of night. Can you imagine how terrifying that would be? On a starless night, in an iron cage, being tumbled down a river. Sheer panic! If you were on the shore with a flashlight and saw someone in this situation, how could you respond with anything other than a massive, spontaneous outflow of compassion—"How can I help you?" Here Tsongkhapa is using the metaphor of the tumbling cage to say, "That's how it is, folks—that's what it's like to be in samsara."

Although we are bound and caged, "still, there are those who have accumulated vast merit over many eons and who have the power of pure aspirations. Therefore, for the sake of those with the fortune," who have the merit "to master," to come to know, "ultimate reality, the treasury of space—by awakening the karmic force of engaging in the action of non-action in great, self-originating, primordial consciousness—I shall present this fundamental king of tantras, spontaneously arisen from the nature of existence of the sugatagarbha."

Up to this point Düdjom Lingpa has written the homage and promised to manifest the text. Now he describes those for whom this text is intended. While the great majority of sentient beings are completely caught up in and bound to the cycle of existence, blindly wandering, there are among these myriad beings some who have tremendous merit, who have made pure prayers over many lifetimes, and, because it may benefit them, Düdjom Lingpa is manifesting this text for them. These fortunate people have something that might be described as karmic force or karmic momentum. The Tibetan term is *létro*. *Lé* is karma; *tro* is something left over, a residue. We could use the metaphor of a cup of water, filled to overflowing, where some of it, something left over, spills over the rim. The term connotes momentum in the sense that our dedication to spiritual practice, the karmic momentum from past lives, is flowing over. It wasn't exhausted in our previous lives, so it is spilling over into this one.

Parents are aware that their children bring something with them into life in terms of personality, behavioral patterns, and so forth. If they arrive with a karmic aptitude for the Dharma derived from activities from previous lives, how is that to be aroused, activated? After all, such a child might be born into an environment where there is nothing that would catalyze that aptitude. They could be born into a family that has no interest whatever in religion, or into a deeply religious family whose beliefs are far from those of Buddhism. There are many possibilities. I know of people for whom their interest in Dharma was only triggered late in life. This is why Tibetan lamas are concerned with identifying *tulkus*—those who have strong karmic momentum for the Dharma from previous lives when they were lamas. It is best to catalyze them as soon as possible, rather than running the risk of their exhausting their positive karmic propensities in the torrent of cyclic existence. In the case of Düdjom Lingpa, his *létro*, his karmic spillover, was watched over by dakinis for the first three years of his life.

"For the sake of those with the fortune," this text is designed to awaken, to arouse this "karmic force." In this sentence we encounter a wonderful paradox: "the action of nonaction." And this nonaction occurs "in great, self-originating," self-manifesting, "primordial consciousness." For those who have the fortune to follow this path, this text is intended to arouse their karmic propensities to engage in Dzogchen, in nonaction. What specifically is nonaction? What is not active? Does this mean that buddha-hood or enlightenment is completely stagnant, static? Of course not. What a farce it would be to declare, "I will become enlightened for the sake of all sentient beings," and then do nothing at all.

When you rest in rigpa, you are nonactive. Even with positive intentions such as "I'm going to do some good for the world; I'm going to help," there is often the subtext of "I'm gonna, I'm gonna," which is doing—ego-driven activity. In rigpa, however, your ego—your reified sense of "I am"—doesn't get to do anything. When resting in rigpa you free up space for another mode of activity to manifest, one that does not arise from the narrow confines of an ego that thinks, "I want this; I don't want that." Rather, it derives from the natural effulgence of ultimate bodhichitta—the effortless, spontaneous, in-the-moment, self-originating expression of dharmakaya. For that to come to the fore we must silence the ego with nonaction. Otherwise the ego is going to take credit for everything.

In presenting "this fundamental king of tantras, spontaneously arisen," Düdjom Lingpa is saying that this is not something he conjured up; this is no treatise that he conceived of and wrote down. Rather, it arose spontaneously from "the nature of existence of the sugatagarbha." Here we encounter another technical term. *Sugata* is an epithet of the Buddha, like *Tathagata*. *Su* is "good," "well," and *gata* is "gone," making "well-gone." *Sugata*, "the one who is well-gone to genuine happiness," is followed by *garbha*, which in Sanskrit has the connotation of "womb," or as the Tibetans translate it, "essence." The *sugatagarbha* is the womb from which all the sugatas have arisen, which is none other than rigpa, our buddha nature.

> Here is how this tantra originated: On the evening of the fifteenth day of the first month of the male water-dog year, by the power of the profound, swift path of the direct crossing-over, the vision of the direct perception of ultimate reality arose. Because I had practiced the path of skillful means of the stage of generation a little, I

reached the ground of a matured vidyadhara. Through that power, all appearances and mental states dissolved into originally pure, ultimate reality, the space of awareness free of conceptual elaboration. Then the very face of the dharmakaya manifested.

This tantra, the *Vajra Essence*, appeared to Düdjom Lingpa in 1862, in February or March of our calendar, on the day of the full moon, "by the power of the profound, swift path of the direct crossing-over." "Crossing-over" is the English translation of *tögal*, the second major phase of Dzogchen practice. It is quite visionary—involving a lot of imagery—and it arises spontaneously from rigpa.

His next phrase, "the vision of the direct perception of ultimate reality arose," is pregnant with meaning. The tögal stage of Dzogchen practice has four major phases of realization, each with a host of correlated experiences and transformations. Whereas in advanced samadhi practices you engage in specific techniques to develop particular siddhis, or paranormal abilities, in the practice of tögal those same siddhis emerge spontaneously. They are exactly the same abilities—walking on water, flying through the air, and so forth—only in tögal they emerge directly from rigpa, like cream rising from milk. Here is a hint as to how powerful these can be: The final, culminating phase of realization in tögal is the *extinction of all phenomena into ultimate reality*. In that experience the universe dissolves into the absolute space of phenomena. The first phase of tögal is called the *direct perception of ultimate reality*. Düdjom Lingpa had this realization when he was twenty-seven years old.

His next line, "Because I had practiced the path of skillful means of the stage of generation a little," is beautifully understated. This is in reference to the stage of generation and the stage of completion, the two main facets of highest-yoga Vajrayana practice. It seems like a very casual statement, yet it is anything but that. Here he hints at something that becomes explicit later in the text: On the Dzogchen path it is not necessary for all individuals to practice the stage of generation to full attainment, nor, having that as a basis, to fully develop in linear fashion the stage of completion, continue on to the first stage of Dzogchen (*tregchö*), and after perfecting that, accomplish tögal. That would be following a developmental model—very linear and sequential.

Tsongkhapa is magnificent in laying out this royal sequence of practices. *Lamrim* (Tibetan for "stages of the path"), using a gradual approach, is the quintessential developmental model and a perfect complement to the *Vajra Essence*, which strongly emphasizes a discovery approach. Dzogchen, following the discovery model, is not so linear. There *are* phases, but it's very clear that if your passion, your calling, is Dzogchen, then some of these sequential, developmental practices may be used essentially to "prime the pump." They are an aid to facilitate the practice. In Dzogchen, drawing from the whole array of tantric practices—stage of generation, deity practices, and so forth—may be very helpful, but you needn't necessarily follow each of them to their culmination.

Düdjom Lingpa refers to this when he says he "practiced the path of skillful means"—the *upaya* side as opposed to the *prajña* side, that is, skillful means as opposed to wisdom. He achieved a direct perception of ultimate reality because he practiced the path of skillful means of the stage of generation, "a little," which means "enough," and thereby, having achieved the vision of the direct perception of ultimate reality, he "reached the ground of a matured vidyadhara." This is the first of four levels of vidyadharas, the final three being a vidyadhara with mastery over life, a Mahamudra vidyadhara, and a spontaneously actualized vidyadhara.

He tells us more of his experience: "Through that power, all appearances and mental states dissolved into originally pure, ultimate reality, the space of awareness free of conceptual elaboration"—in other words, they dissolved into emptiness. Then, being a Vajrayana practitioner, a Dzogchen adept, he not only realized emptiness, but in that open spaciousness, "the very face of the dharmakaya manifested." He ascertained buddha nature. There is more to the experience of buddha nature than the realization of emptiness. The realization of emptiness prepares the way to recognize your own face, your own nature, as the dharmakaya.

After some time, the following spontaneous appearances arose in the form of a buddhafield:

On that very occasion of self-originating, originally pure, great
bliss, my environment naturally arose as the actual Akanishta...

Before we go into this extraordinary vision, let's examine the mind to which
such appearances might arise in order to be clear about its nature. We can
establish a three-dimensional model of the mind. First there is the psyche,
typified by dualistic thinking, imagination, personal history, and so forth—
the subject matter of psychology. The psyche is also called the *ordinary
mind*, and, in Sanskrit, *chitta*. The psyche emerges from what Sogyal Rinpoche calls the "ground of the ordinary mind."

The Sanskrit term for this second layer, this ground of the ordinary
mind, is *alayavijñana*, which is translated as the "substrate consciousness."
(This corresponds closely to the Theravada Buddhist term *bhavanga*, or
"ground of becoming.") That ground, from which your individual psyche
emerges, is not the brain. The substrate consciousness carries over from
lifetime to lifetime, so its existence doesn't depend on the brain you have
in this or any other lifetime. Your individual psyche will be finished once
you have died. But it will have left imprints in your substrate consciousness. It is there that your karma, your talents, your proclivities, and so
forth are stored, much as information is stored in electromagnetic fields
when sending emails from one computer to another using wireless internet. So the substrate consciousness is deeper than the psyche, but it is still
not buddha nature, which is the third and most profound level in our
three-tiered model.

We tap into the substrate consciousness at times quite naturally, without effort, without our having to be a great yogi. This happens, for
instance, in dreamless sleep, which usually occurs several times every
twenty-four hours. In the dreamless state of deep sleep, mental activities
become dormant and we slip into the substrate consciousness. Because our
awareness is dull rather than luminous, we don't receive much benefit
except for a good night's sleep. We also experience the substrate consciousness at the time of death. We need to be clear here—this is not the
"clear light of death." The ground of the ordinary mind, the substrate consciousness, is not "ground awareness"—synonymous with buddha nature,

rigpa, and dharmakaya. The ground of the ordinary mind is individual, conditioned, and linear within time—it is within the causal nexus.

In the dying process the senses shut down one by one. They retract. The
tentacles of awareness withdraw from the five physical senses back into
mental awareness, where you still have imagination, thoughts, feelings, and
so forth. And then, as you are withdrawing, the derivative mental processes
of feeling, discernment, memory, imagination, recognition, and so on are
also withdrawn. The dying person experiences images of light—white light
and red light—so some mental imagery arises, and then that too goes. After
that you literally lose your mind when you experience the "black near-
attainment," which is a kind of blackout. This is an experience similar to
going under general anesthesia. Here the mind hasn't become completely
extinguished, simply disappearing into nothing. Rather, the coarse mind
has become utterly dormant by dissolving into the ground of ordinary
mind, leaving no vestiges of imagery, personal history, or ego.

Most people, when they enter that phase of the dying process, simply
black out—they have no recognition of anything. Next, they emerge from
that blackout directly into the clear light of death, which is the primordial
ground underlying the ground of the ordinary mind. Everyone has that.
Then, once the clear light of death passes, it's over—"you" are gone—and
the body begins to decompose.

Comparing the two—the ordinary ground of the mind (*alayavijñana*)
and the clear light of death (*rigpa, dharmakaya*)—I would characterize the
former as a relative vacuum state of consciousness and the latter as the
absolute vacuum state of consciousness. They are not the same; they are
qualitatively different, and they need to be distinguished. How do you
achieve the former apart from falling into deep sleep or dying? How do
you deliberately gain access to the ground of the ordinary mind? By way
of meditative quiescence—shamatha. That is what shamatha is good for.

The substrate consciousness, a relative vacuum state of consciousness,
is implicitly structured by concepts but has enormous potential. That
potential—in terms of creativity—is revealed in deep hypnosis, which is
another situation where you are very close to the ground state of the ordinary
mind. We know that hypnosis can be used to break strong habits such as

smoking. Furthermore a person can be convinced that an onion tastes like an apple, or can be made to believe that he or she is some kind of animal. (I recall seeing a demonstration on television where a man was convinced he was a kangaroo and hopped around the stage with a contented smile on his face.) In such circumstances the mind is unusually flexible because it is in a mode of great potentiality as opposed to its normal state of manifestation.

In like manner, if you wish to develop mundane siddhis—paranormal abilities, extrasensory perception—shamatha is the basis to bring forth, to manifest, that potential. Attaining such abilities can be extremely beneficial, as the great eleventh-century Indian mahasiddha Atisha made clear, saying, "The merit gained in a single day by someone with extrasensory perception cannot be gained even in a hundred lifetimes by someone without extrasensory perception."[4] In the same commentary he said that by achieving shamatha you can attain extrasensory perception. Therefore, if you want to tap into the full potential of your individual mindstream, train in shamatha. Of course you might see a danger there. Someone with just enough of an ethical constitution to achieve shamatha could develop shamatha and nothing else, thus tapping into something very deep and very powerful. Is it possible that this person might become a narcissistic, megalomaniac, "siddhi-worker," impressing people with paranormal abilities, exhibiting a gargantuan, pseudo-divine pride, based on the belief "I am number one"? Might this person delve into black magic and engage in evil activities? Fortunately, there's a catch.

In fact, you cannot develop or maintain shamatha with a malicious motivation. To achieve shamatha you must overcome the five types of obscurations, one of which is ill will, enmity, or malice. You cannot carry that baggage into shamatha, because it's just antithetical to the practice. Such obscurations have to go, because the full achievement of shamatha is, by definition, a sublime state that brings with it exceptional mental balance. It is the epitome of mental health.

Bearing in mind that your mental afflictions have not been permanently eliminated by shamatha, what would happen if, having achieved shamatha, you fell prey to an affliction such as jealousy? As soon as that comes up, your samadhi diminishes. This is built into the nature of the mind—you cannot have malice and the wish to apply shamatha-derived siddhis, thereby using them in an evil manner.

The great historical example is that of Devadatta, the Buddha's cousin. Devadatta had achieved not merely shamatha, which is access to the first dhyana; he had displayed siddhis arising from having achieved all four dhyanas.[5] He did not have deep insight into vipashyana, however, which irreversibly purifies the mind of all its afflictions, such as craving, hostility, and delusion. Jealous of the Buddha's royal patrons, Devadatta decided to impress the king by using his siddhis to catch the king's attention. He succeeded, but the Buddha had a far greater following, and Devadatta couldn't bear that. So he plotted with the equally jealous prince—this king's son. The prince would kill his father, and Devadatta would do away with Buddha, and then Devadatta would become head of the Sangha (the Buddhist congregation), and the prince would become the king, and they would work together. As soon as Devadatta got on that track, however, his siddhis vanished.

I mention this in order to demonstrate that there is enormous creativity, enormous potential, in the ground of the ordinary mind, the substrate consciousness. There is infinitely more potential if you arrive at this ground and on that basis practice vipashyana, the stage of generation, the breakthrough (tregchö), and the direct crossing-over (tögal). The creative potential there is simply limitless, and that is what is being described here. Rather than a hypnotic state, a dream, or even a lucid dream manifesting from the ground of the ordinary mind, this "ground of a matured vidyadhara" is tapping into the deepest ground state. What then specifically manifested from Düdjom Lingpa's dwelling in the rigpa of a vidyadhara?

There are many pure lands with their related deities—Tara, Avalokiteshvara, and so forth. Akanishta is the pure realm, the buddhafield associated with Samantabhadra, the Primordial Buddha. Furthermore, it is the pure land in which all beings finally achieve buddhahood. Whether your ordinary body is located in Bodhgaya or in Hollywood, this buddhafield is where you have your final meditation before achieving enlightenment. From the first-person perspective you are in Akanishta. Here is what it will look like, as far as words can portray it to people who are not enlightened. Visualize it. Use your imagination.

THE VISION OF DÜDJOM LINGPA

> This magically displayed buddhafield was vast and spacious, and its
> surface was smooth, level, and pliant to the touch. Grassy mountains
> of medicinal herbs were fragrant with mists of pleasing aromas. The
> whole ground was completely covered with various radiant, lumi-
> nous, clear, sparkling, shimmering, lovely flowers in shades of white,
> yellow, red, green, blue, and variegated hues. In the four directions
> were four oceans of ambrosia imbued with eight excellent qualities.
> On the shores of those great oceans were pebbles of jewels, sands
> of gold, turquoise meadows, and overarching halos of rainbows.

There are eight qualities of ambrosia, which are the eight qualities of excellent water. As far as words can capture it, the eight qualities of pure water,
or ambrosia, are: cool, sweet, light, soft, clear, soothing, pleasant, and
wholesome. With pure vision, in contrast to our ordinary view, pure water
and even ordinary water is ambrosia. The relativity of the qualities of water
is reflected in the classic explanation that a glass of water seen by a hungry
ghost appears as pus, to a human being as ordinary water, and by a god it
is seen as ambrosia.

> Forests of wish-fulfilling trees flourished in the four cardinal direc-
> tions, billowing forth clouds of sensory offerings. Various types of
> beautiful, apparitional birds voiced the sounds of Dharma with gen-
> tle, soothing calls. Various lovely, emanated animals frolicked about
> and appeared to be contentedly listening to the Dharma. The whole
> sky was covered with checkered patterns of lattices of rainbow light.
> Everywhere the sky was filled with singing and dancing viras and
> virahs, while many goddesses made sensory offerings and expressed
> their devotion.

Viras are male and *virahs* are female. The etymology is "heroic," or "hero,"
so the Sanskrit here refers to male and female heroic beings. Gyatrul Rinpoche comments that viras are male and virahs are female bodhisattvas,

manifesting in the world in order to be of service to other beings. They have the courage to encounter, confront, and overwhelm mental afflictions.

> In the center of this region, in a great, delightful garden, resting against a tree covered with foliage and flowers, a vast and lofty jeweled throne was supported by eight lions. The branches of the tree were draped with various silk hangings, jeweled lattices and half-lattices, and many tinkling miniature bells ringing with the natural sounds of the holy Dharma.
>
> Upon this lion-supported throne was a seat composed of a lotus, sun, and moon, upon which sat the true Teacher, Samantabhadra, the Lake-Born Vajra, appearing naturally with the radiance of the ground of reality. His body was indigo in color, bearing the features of an eight-year-old youth. His right hand was in the mudra of expounding the Dharma, and his left hand was in the mudra of meditative equipoise. He was adorned with the signs and symbols of enlightenment and all the apparel of the sambhogakaya. Within the realm of his oceanic, radiant, transparent body, all the peaceful and wrathful buddhas and myriads of buddhafields and emanations naturally appeared, like planets and stars reflected brightly in a lake. Innumerable rays of blazing light emanated from him, and from their tips appeared various symbolic letters.

"The Lake-Born Vajra" refers to Samantabhadra emanating as Padmasambhava. "The radiance of the ground of reality" is the luminosity of buddha nature itself. "The signs and symbols of enlightenment" are the thirty-two major signs and the eighty minor symbols on the body that are characteristic of a fully enlightened being. This is a pure vision that is accessible only to arya-bodhisattvas, meaning that the person experiencing this is a vidyadhara and has had the direct perception of ultimate reality. These beings have direct access to the sambhogakaya. Here the universe with its multiple buddhafields and buddhas—vast, ocean-like emanations—is seen within the body of the true Teacher. Having set the scene, Düdjom Lingpa now describes the assembly:

Gathered around the Teacher, a magically displayed retinue of 84,000 disciples was assembled, including Bodhisattva Vajra of Awareness, Bodhisattva Faculty of Wisdom, Bodhisattva Vajra of Primordial Consciousness, Bodhisattva Boundless Great Emptiness, Bodhisattva Faculty of Pervasive Luminosity, Bodhisattva Spontaneous Display, Bodhisattva Lord of External Appearances, Bodhisattva Faculty of Vision, Bodhisattva Faculty of Hearing, Bodhisattva Faculty of Smell, Bodhisattva Faculty of Taste, Bodhisattva Faculty of Touch, and more. They were all looking at the Teacher while sitting silently, bowed in reverence. The Teacher was also silent as he gazed into the expanse of the sky. At that moment, the natural sound of ultimate reality emerged from the absolute domain of pristine space:

Ah!
The whole of samsara and nirvana is groundless and rootless.
The Vajra Queen is great space.
The great emptiness of space is the Great Mother.
All phenomena are apparitions
of ultimate reality and the one nature of existence.
Everything arises from the unborn.
The emerging apparitions cease.
Causes and conditions are extinguished right where they are.
Thus, in ultimate reality, the Teacher and the teaching,
the path and its fruition, are devoid of signs and words.
The many avenues of skillful means and wisdom
appear as a great natural occurrence and natural arising.
The space of nonobjectivity and great openness
is limpid, clear, and free of contamination.
All displays of the buddhafield, Teacher, and retinue
are nonexistent, but from nonexistence they appear as existent.
How we praise this with great wonder!

The magically displayed retinue is gathered around the Teacher, Samanta-bhadra. *Ah* is the symbol of emptiness. Therefore, "groundless and root-less," the whole of samsara and nirvana is apparitional; it is not grounded in anything inherently existing. It can be compared to a rainbow or a magical display—there is nothing really there. The whole of samsara and nirvana is not really anywhere. "All displays of the buddhafield, Teacher, and ret-inue are nonexistent" in the sense of being "not inherently existent."

TEACHER AND ASSEMBLY IN DIALOGUE

> As soon as this sound arose, the entire assembled retinue spoke with one voice to the Bhagavan, "O Teacher, Bhagavan, Omnipresent Lord, and Immutable Sovereign, please listen to us and consider our words! Please, Teacher, explain why this entire buddhafield is here, with Teacher and assembled disciples, and tell us how this arose."

Bhagavan is a Sanskrit epithet of the Buddha. The term suggests "Lord," denoting someone with supreme qualities of freedom from obscurations, perfection of virtues, and transcendence from samsara.

> The Teacher replied, "O apparitional disciples who have magically appeared and gathered here, listen: You ask why these magical dis-plays of primordial consciousness—the buddhafield, Teacher, and disciples—have arisen. They are for the sake of revealing an entrance to the nonconceptual primordial consciousness of the mind of all the sugatas of the three times, who manifest in accordance with the faculties of all the beings wandering in the three realms of samsara. By the great power of wisdom and primordial consciousness, the natural emergence of the actual Akanishta as a buddhafield is revealed in the great vision of ultimate reality. As for myself, the Teacher is the primordial ground, which naturally appears to itself from the innate radiance of the sugatagarbha. The natural radiance of empty awareness, free of conceptual elaboration, appears as Bodhisattva Vajra of Awareness. The natural radiance of the wisdom

of identitylessness appears as Bodhisattva Faculty of Wisdom. The
natural radiance of the eight kinds of consciousness, together with
the mental factors, appears as the assembled retinue."

This visionary experience—the manifestation of the buddhafield Akanishta—
is a means to reveal ultimate reality, which is beyond all ordinary physical
form. Bodhisattva Vajra of Awareness, one of the individuals in the retinue,
is an expression of the natural radiance of empty awareness taking on symbolically an archetypal form as a person. We will hear from him later. Bodhisattva Faculty of Wisdom is another character in the extensive assembly who
will pose questions to the Buddha, the Teacher, Samantabhadra.

What are the "eight kinds of consciousness" mentioned in the last line?
More often we hear of the *six* kinds of consciousness—the five sensory
modes of consciousness plus mental consciousness. In Dzogchen two more
are added to this list. The seventh, called *afflictive cognition*, is the mind's natural potency of the darkness of ignorance and delusion. Within the context
of Dzogchen this mode—grasping on to *I am* and then grasping on to aversion, craving, and so forth—is considered so important that it has its own
category. The eighth, which we visited earlier, is the substrate consciousness: the ground out of which the psyche and all of the ordinary manifestations of the mind emerge and into which they dissolve.

The natural radiance of the eight kinds of consciousness, together with
mental factors, appears as the "assembled retinue." This is reminiscent of
a term from modern sociology: the society of mind.[6] This retinue is a
truly noble society of mind. Here we find all the 84,000 components of
the mind (according to the classic Buddhist formulation) manifesting as
bodhisattvas, each having its own voice, its own perspective, and all of
this is taking place in the dharmakaya realm, with Samantabhadra, a.k.a.
Padmasambhava, presiding. These bodhisattvas, these sublimated manifestations of your ordinary mind, then pose questions to your own buddha
nature: "Oh Teacher, Bhagavan, please explain this," sometimes debating,
sometimes probing, at other times disagreeing. The ordinary mind is
wrestling with buddha nature! This drama arises spontaneously from the
dharmakaya.

"The natural radiance of the eight kinds of consciousness, together with the mental processes, appears as the assembled retinue." This line concludes what are called the preparatory sections of the text, which are, classically: homage, the commitment to compose or reveal the text, and a designation of the disciples or students for whom the text is intended. Also, since this is a mind terma, Düdjom Lingpa has described the manner in which it emerged. This, as we have seen, is unlike the majority of cases where someone requests a text and the author writes it.

2

THE QUESTIONS OF FACULTY OF WISDOM

The scene has now been set for the main body of the *Vajra Essence*. The first section concerns the questions raised by the bodhisattva Faculty of Wisdom. As their names suggest, the bodhisattvas who engage with Samantabhadra in this text are embodiments of the different mental factors and capacities of the human mind.

> Then Bodhisattva Faculty of Wisdom rose from his seat and asked the Bhagavan, "O Teacher, Bhagavan, you appear as the natural radiance of the sugatagarbha. I, Faculty of Wisdom, appear as the natural radiance of wisdom. Vajra of Awareness appears as the natural radiance of awareness. The assembly of male and female bodhisattvas appears as the eight kinds of consciousness, together with the mental factors. But if this is so, we should appear in that way to all the beings of the three realms. Therefore, why do they carry on in the midst of the delusive appearances of joys, sorrows, friends, and enemies in the three realms of existence, where miseries occur and pure appearances do not? Teacher, please explain!"

Sugatagarbha—in a manner of speaking, the "womb of all the buddhas"—is something utterly central, primordial, and cosmic. The teacher Samantabhadra arises as the natural radiance of the sugatagarbha, whereas Faculty of Wisdom recognizes himself as an emanation, or embodiment, of wisdom.

Here a distinction must be made between primordial consciousness (*jñana*), often translated as *primordial wisdom*, and *wisdom* (*prajña*). The latter is something that is cultivated. You meditate diligently, you practice vipashyana, stage of generation, and so forth, and then wisdom is aroused, or generated. Wisdom in this context is developmental—you have a little bit now and then later you have more.

In contrast, you never have more or less primordial consciousness, because its nature is primordial, making it more like intuition. You don't really generate intuition. You can clarify it and you can learn to distinguish genuine intuition from conceptual superimpositions, preferences, hopes, fears, and expectations—things that can be very easily conflated with intuition. When your true intuition speaks, it speaks clearly, distinctly, like a bell, rather than as a cacophony of multiple voices leaving you to wonder which one was intuition and which was just mental processes churning away out of habitual predilections.

Vajra of Awareness refers to a primordial, pristine awareness that is immutable, adamantine, indestructible, changeless—the nature of a vajra. In this context, where there is no accompanying adjective such as "pristine," "pure," or "original," *awareness* means rigpa. Thus Vajra of Awareness appears as the natural radiance of rigpa.

The entire assembly of male and female bodhisattvas appears from, or is a manifestation of, the eight kinds of consciousness (which, as we saw previously, are the five sensory consciousnesses, mental consciousness, afflictive consciousness, and the substrate consciousness) "together with the mental factors." There are fifty-one mental factors, or processes that occur within an individual's mind, such as feeling, discrimination, and intention.

Using pure vision, Bodhisattva Faculty of Wisdom sees right through the outward display of these different apparitional disciples of the retinue of Samantabhadra to what they symbolize. Then he is asking, if this is their actual nature, if these bodhisattvas are simply the natural radiance of the properties of awareness, shouldn't they appear in that way to all the beings of the three realms? Why doesn't everyone see them this way? Why do beings persist "in the midst of the delusive appearances of joys, sorrows, friends, and enemies in the three realms of existence, where miseries occur and pure appearances do not?" If these appearances are "delusive," why don't the beings of the three realms see this? What's wrong here? "Teacher, please explain!"

> He replied, "O noble one, beings that have slipped into the ethically neutral ground do not see pure appearances. Impure, delusive mental states and appearances of friends, enemies, joys, and sorrows are characteristic of ordinary sentient beings.

The "ethically neutral ground" is a dimension of consciousness that is neither virtuous nor nonvirtuous, and so it is called *ethically neutral*. Furthermore, because it is the subtle stream of mental consciousness from which the psyche emerges, it is called *ground*. The Tibetan term translated as "ethically neutral" (*lung ma ten*) refers to something that is neither meritorious nor deleterious—something unspecified and neutral. In and of themselves, ethically neutral actions create virtually no karmic imprints. They won't lead to a fortunate rebirth or a miserable rebirth; they take you neither toward enlightenment nor away from it. That is the nature of the *alayavijñana*. Thus "ethically neutral ground" is another phrase for the *alayavijñana*, the ground of the ordinary mind, the substrate consciousness spoken of earlier. The *alayavijñana*, when you settle into it, is radiantly clear but is not in itself a virtuous state of mind.

Most beings periodically slip into and out of this ethically neutral ground: into the *alayavijñana*—as in the case of deep sleep, the blackout period when dying, or when we achieve shamatha—then out, where we can do a lot of damage or a lot of good. This is the whole nature of our existence. This is what it means to be "cycling continuously in samsara," whether it is from moment to moment or from lifetime to lifetime. When you enter the ethically neutral ground, the ego has become dormant. Therefore no virtue is created, nor any vice. You have reached the ground of the ordinary mind, but you have not tapped into the ultimate ground, primordial consciousness.

In contrast, what highly realized beings such as vidyadharas do is to slip in and out of the luminous, self-knowing experience of primordial consciousness. They don't merely tap into the *alayavijñana*, they break through all of the reified, preconscious structuring—the karmic residue of that ethically neutral ground. They shatter that and enter the vast expanse. Vidyadharas periodically ascertain this ground of awareness— the ultimate virtue from which all relative virtues spring—then they manifest in the world with pure vision, with divine pride, and then dissolve back into primordial consciousness once again. Their practice is simply an oscillation between primordial consciousness and pure vision until they reach buddhahood, at which point they attain a nonabiding state of enlightenment, meaning they no longer dwell in the duality of samsara and nirvana.

"Beings that have slipped into the ethically neutral ground" may imagine pure appearances, but they don't actually see them. Instead they experience "impure"— meaning tainted by mental afflictions: aversion, craving, delusion, and so forth, which invite further delusion, creating a vicious cycle—"delusive mental states and appearances of friends, enemies" (which indicates demarcation; our fellow sentient beings are being categorized) and "joys, and sorrows." This is life in samsara: We oscillate between joys and sorrows, encountering friends and enemies, along with numerous other beings that mean little to us.

THE APPEARANCE OF TEACHERS

"By the great power of wisdom and primordial consciousness, inconceivable pure appearances arise here to individuals who have previously sat in the presence of the nonhuman, naturally appearing Teacher, the perfect Buddha Orgyen Lake-Born Vajra. These people have attained the supreme siddhi after entering the gateway of Vajrayana Dharma and applying themselves diligently to its practice. From then until the myriad realms of beings are empty, due to the power of their pure aspirations, they repeatedly appear as teachers for the sake of the world, teaching in accordance with the individual needs of disciples.

These inconceivable pure appearances arise by the great power of *wisdom*, that is, *prajña*, which is cultivated, and of *primordial consciousness*, which is discovered, or unveiled. These appearances arise to individuals who have sat in the presence of "the nonhuman, naturally appearing Teacher, the perfect Buddha Orgyen Lake-Born Vajra."

In the Pali canon, the first recorded teachings of the Buddha Shakyamuni, the Buddha actually said, "I'm not human." To be a buddha, even if you entered our world with a human body, is to transcend species. A buddha not only transcends species, but also transcends the three realms—the desire, form, and formless realms. An awakened one is no longer categorized in any of these ways. Thus the retinue is seated before the *"nonhuman,* naturally appearing, perfect Buddha Orgyen Lake-Born Vajra," who is a manifestation of Padmasambhava. This retinue sees with pure vision, sees things the way they really are.

After having entered into the Vajrayana Dharma and having applied themselves diligently, these people have attained the "supreme siddhi," that is, enlightenment. Then, "until the myriad realms of beings are empty" and "due to the power of their pure aspirations," they return as teachers, "teaching in accordance with the individual needs," capacities, dispositions, and so forth, of disciples. This is reminiscent of the prayer with which His Holiness the Dalai Lama often ends his teachings, which is from Shantideva's *Guide to the Bodhisattva Way of Life*: "For as long as space remains, for as long as sentient beings remain, so long shall I remain to alleviate the suffering of the world."[7]

> "When their previous karmic predispositions stir, they directly see the truth of ultimate reality, and they emerge from the realm of wisdom. Pure appearances arise for them, but these are neither the mind nor mental processes. Rather, these appearances are by nature the play of the manifest space of awareness. They are not the eight kinds of consciousness, but they are not otherwise, so they are called by these names. These appearances arise in numerous ways from the nondual Teacher and retinue. Those known as bodhisattvas have gone well beyond mundane existence, even

though they have not become buddhas; that is why they are so known."

The "previous karmic predispositions" that stir or manifest are those of students who have come under the guidance of these enlightened beings who appear in accordance with the students' needs. These students then see "the truth of ultimate reality," that is, they are elevated, becoming themselves vidyadharas, "and they emerge from the realm of wisdom." Having been drenched, immersed in that realization of emptiness, you emerge as an illusory being, knowing that you have never been anything other than an expression of dharmakaya, the mind of the Buddha. "Pure appearances arise for them" spontaneously once they have tapped into the ultimate ground and seen it in an unmediated fashion. The pure appearances that arise for those who have been led to the state of a vidyadhara emerge as they engage with conventional reality, but these are neither the ordinary mind, nor are they the ordinary mental processes. They are not equivalent to those since they have now gained access to something far deeper.

For clarification let's refer to the three-tiered model of the mind presented earlier. The first and most superficial level is the psyche, in which thoughts, fantasies, images, and so forth appear. If you sit quietly and watch your mind, the phenomena you observe manifest in your psyche. We access the second level, the substrate consciousness, in deep sleep, the blackout period of death, and in the practice of shamatha. During shamatha meditation the phenomena observed do not necessarily emanate solely from the psyche, which is encapsulated within this lifetime. Having accessed the substrate consciousness, there is the potential for tapping into memories from past lifetimes, phenomena entangled within a vast network of experiences. These may appear in the form of dreams, visions, desires, or fears whose origin is not to be found in this lifetime. In the case of fear, for example, the anxiety may be very real, yet its origin may be a past-life experience. Such fear is an expression of imprints stored in the substrate consciousness.

Then, having broken through to the third tier of the mind—primordial consciousness—what emerges, the phenomena that appear, are not manifestations of mind and mental processes. From this deeper vantage point, such manifestations and mental processes, which comprise the psyche, are surface phenomena. For the same reason it would also be misleading to depict these primordial experiences as manifestations of the substrate consciousness. Appearances originating in primordial consciousness are the spontaneous, natural effulgence of pristine awareness. Being neither the mind nor mental processes, "these appearances are by nature the play of the manifest space of awareness"—dharmadhatu.

How can these pure appearances not be the eight kinds of consciousness while also being "not otherwise"? It would be inaccurate to describe the eight kinds of consciousness as being "over here" whereas pure appearances are "over there" because from the viewpoint of primordial consciousness, they are nondual. For example, if you truly fathom the nature of anger as it arises—even something as slight as a mild irritation—it is seen to be nothing other than an expression of pristine awareness. Of course we don't normally do that. We grasp on to anger, reify it, and then act out within the sphere of the psyche and of ordinary appearances, in which case anger is an afflictive emotion. Therefore, if you fathom the nature of the mental processes—the eight kinds of consciousness—it is seen that they have never been anything other than expressions of primordial consciousness. However, not fathoming their nature, they are then seen either as expressions of the substrate consciousness or expressions of the psyche, indicating that you are locked within samsara.

Even so, some terminology must be applied to speak of them, "so they are called by these names"—the "eight kinds of consciousness." Something similar happens in physics. These appearances, the play of the manifest space of awareness, that "arise in numerous ways from the nondual Teacher and retinue," are appearances of pure vision.

The last line of this paragraph explains the difference between bodhisattvas and buddhas. A bodhisattva—although having gone "well beyond mundane existence"—is someone still on the path to buddhahood. "That is why they are so known" as bodhisattvas and not yet buddhas. Once you arrive at the culmination of the path, you have the freedom, if you so choose, to manifest as a bodhisattva.

Again Bodhisattva Faculty of Wisdom spoke: "Yes, O Teacher, Bhagavan. If the mystically displayed Teacher and the entire retinue are nondual, and not different, as you have said, there is no purpose for all the teaching and listening on the part of the Teacher and the assembly of disciples. Since there is no difference in the quality of everyone's primordial consciousness, what is the point in putting on a show of teaching and listening? Teacher, please explain!"

He replied, "O Faculty of Wisdom, the naturally appearing teacher known as Shakyamuni arose as an emanation for disciples in the past, like sunlight from the sun. The Teacher, those who sought teachings from him, and the retinue, acting as listeners, appeared to be teaching or listening to individual kinds of spiritual paths and vehicles for training disciples. Although the Teacher and the retinue were nondual, for the sake of the disciples, various expressions of skillful means were displayed, like a magician and his magic."

Faculty of Wisdom's question makes sense. If both parties are of the same nature, "since there is no difference in the quality of everyone's primordial consciousness," why put on a "show of teaching and listening"? In answer, the Bhagavan introduces a historical precedent. The teachings of Shakyamuni usually took place in the context of the Buddha and someone who approached him either with a question or with a request for a certain type of teaching or guidance. At times he would address a single individual and at other times he would teach a small circle of disciples or larger groups in the dozens, or hundreds, on up to thousands. In many cases the roles were: teacher, requestor, and those listening to the teaching, the disciples. The teacher and the retinue were nondual from a *buddha's perspective*, an enlightened perspective. Viewed from primordial consciousness, all were nondual; no one among them was essentially less enlightened than any of the others.

This setting of the teacher and disciples exemplifies the intersection of ultimate and conventional reality. From the dharmakaya perspective, the Buddha and his disciples, his students, have always been enlightened; all are simply manifestations of buddha mind. That is the ultimate truth. The students' perspective, however, is grounded in conventional truth.

There is a tendency, which I've encountered often as a teacher, for students to go overboard when they encounter the discovery model, the perspective of buddha nature, primordial consciousness, and the teachings of Dzogchen. It seems so easy, spontaneous, and refreshing that they fall in love with it. By contrast, the developmental model comes to seem mechanical, linear, and dualistic, so students then tend to pull away from that. In doing so they reject conventional reality and the many techniques for transforming the mind. We could read this propensity into Faculty of Wisdom's words. He is saying, in effect, "All right, if we are all nondual, if we are all of the same nature—why bother with teachings and practice? Since everything is of the nature of dharmakaya, there is no point in doing anything whatsoever because everyone is already enlightened."

The Teacher then provides a more balanced perspective. Viewed from the dharmakaya—from absolute reality—the Buddha has never been anything other than a buddha, and his disciples are merely manifestations of buddha mind. On the other hand, from the perspective of sentient beings and conventional truth, "for the sake of the disciples, various expressions of skillful means were displayed, like a magician and his magic." So ultimate reality and conventional reality are of the same nature—nondual—two aspects of the same reality viewed from different perspectives.

3

THE QUESTIONS OF GREAT BOUNDLESS EMPTINESS

Bodhisattva Boundless Emptiness now questions the Teacher. In Sanskrit, Boundless Emptiness is *Mahashunyananta*. *Maha* is "great"; *shunya* is "empty"; *ananta* is "limitless, boundless." Therefore, the name of this bodhisattva means "great emptiness, vast and limitless."

> Then Bodhisattva Boundless Emptiness reverently bowed to the Bhagavan, and joining his palms, asked, "O Teacher, Bhagavan, so that all beings may be liberated from the ocean of miseries of mundane existence and reach the state of liberation, please grant us the profound pith instructions to actually achieve the state of the fully perfected Buddha Samantabhadra in one lifetime and with one body."

First, why do we need any teachings at all? We need them because not everyone knows that he or she is a buddha. Therefore these teachings are given so that skillful means may be used to reveal to us our own buddha nature. Needless to say the activities of someone like Düdjom Lingpa, who is the fifteenth incarnation of Buddha's disciple Shariputra, may be a bit beyond our reach. Understanding this, Düdjom Lingpa then presents the practices upon which he wants us to focus, practices that he makes clear are not beyond us.

Here the bodhisattva is requesting those teachings that are most effective, those that lead most swiftly to the realization of perfect buddhahood. The entire *Vajra Essence* is basically in answer to this initial question posed by Bodhisattva Great Boundless Emptiness. At the end, the author, Düdjom Lingpa, says that if achieving buddhahood is your interest, you needn't look outside of this text. The *Vajra Essence* has all of the information that you need. He doesn't say that you shouldn't look outside this text—of course you can. But this text contains all of the knowledge, the guidance necessary. Of course having a teacher to guide you through these practices would help.

THE SWIFT PATH—THE GREAT PERFECTION

> The Teacher replied, "O Great Boundless Emptiness and the rest of you assembled here, listen! The great, sublime path that brings all sentient beings to the stages and paths of liberation is called the swift path of the clear light Great Perfection.

The word for teacher here means a revealer, one who reveals, who shows what needs to be known. *Stages* and *paths* are technical terms with precise, detailed meanings. The Sanskrit term translated as "stage" is *bhumi*, which literally means "ground." Within the Mahayana teachings there are five paths—the path of accumulation, the path of preparation, the path of seeing, the path of meditation, and the path of no more training. They are sequential and provide a general roadmap to enlightenment, but they require three countless eons.[8] The Mahayana path of accumulation begins when bodhichitta arises spontaneously in your mindstream and you thereby become a bodhisattva. The path of preparation is characterized by a gradual deepening of insight into emptiness. The Mahayana path of seeing begins with the bodhisattva's initial nondual, nonconceptual realization of emptiness. In the path of meditation you oscillate back and forth between a state of complete absorption in meditation on emptiness and a state where you manifest as an illusory being, realizing the dreamlike nature of all phenomena. This is likened to repeatedly soaking clothes in water and then removing them, a process of washing out even the subtlest stains. Having come to the end of the path of meditation you go on to achieve the path of no more training.

There are different approaches to these five paths. You may follow the shravaka path as taught in the Pali canon and many Sanskrit sutras. At the culmination of the five paths you achieve nirvana, becoming an arhat. Another approach is the path of the solitary realizers, the pratyekabuddhas. Although they will receive teachings at times during their many lifetimes on the way to liberation, they come to the culmination of their path on their own. During periods that are spiritually barren, out of their compassion and concern for the world, pratyekabuddhas manifest to inspire others on the path to liberation. In such degenerate periods people simply cannot be reached by oral teachings, their ears and hearts are closed. Such teachers may be able to rattle the cage of people's self-conceptual imprisonment, however, by displaying siddhis. Pratyekabuddhas, then, follow five paths that are somewhat distinct from the five paths of the shravakas, and it takes longer to proceed along that route.

Finally there are the five paths of the bodhisattvas, including the ten *bhumis*, the arya-bodhisattva stages that begin on the Mahayana path of seeing, when direct realization of emptiness is first experienced. So when you first become a bodhisattva you embark on the Mahayana path of accumulation, and that is followed by the path of preparation, which entails deeper insight, and deeper bodhichitta. Next is the path of seeing. As a bodhisattva, on first achieving nondual realization of emptiness, of ultimate reality, you become an arya-bodhisattva. On having that realization and entering the path of seeing, you reach the first bhumi. Then the next nine bhumis are stages of exponential growth culminating in the achievement of perfect enlightenment.

The first seven of these bhumis are called "impure" because the mind is still tainted by mental afflictions (*kleshas*). Although at this point these obscurations are pretty weak, they've not been completely expunged. The overall format of practice at this stage is to alternate—first soaking your awareness in the unmediated realization of emptiness and then coming out and engaging in the bountiful, virtuous deeds of a bodhisattva. In meditation you experience *prajña*, wisdom, and then emerge practicing *upaya*, skillful means, accumulating vast stores of merit that carry the taste of your realization of emptiness. From that point on, having experienced an unmediated realization of ultimate reality, you can never be compelled to take birth in any lower realm and you no longer accumulate propulsive karma—the kind that hurtles ordinary sentient beings from one life to the next. You can voluntarily choose your rebirths. There is still the need to return to samsara because there is unfinished work, but the choice of rebirth is guided by wisdom and compassion: "Where can I be of greatest benefit? Where can I find suitable teachers to guide me further along the path?"

On the first seven impure bhumis the mind is gradually purified, the *afflictive obscurations* becoming subtler and subtler, until you arrive at the eighth bhumi. This is the first pure bhumi, at which point *kleshas* have been eliminated. You have now cut the root of samsara and experience the same freedom as an arhat, but your wisdom, compassion, and other virtues are far greater. At that point it would be impossible for you to become angry or experience any of the other afflictive obscurations. It doesn't matter what terrible things people might do to you or what desirable object you might see. All tendencies of delusion, hostility, craving, pride, and envy have vanished. What still lingers are extremely subtle obscurations, the cognitive obscurations, which are all that stands between you and the completely unimpeded awareness of a buddha.

You begin to overcome those extremely subtle obscurations on the eighth bhumi, a process of purification that continues on the ninth and tenth bhumis. Then you enter the path of no more training, where you achieve the vajra-like *samadhi* and attain buddhahood. You go from the unimaginably vast mind of a bodhisattva on the tenth bhumi until finally the bubble of the subtlest obscurations bursts, and the limitless potential of primordial consciousness is unveiled. At that point there is nothing more for you to do in terms of your own purification. To sum up, for the bodhisattva there are the paths of accumulation, preparation, seeing, and then the nine bhumis of the path of meditation, all culminating in the path of no more training, which for the Mahayana path is buddhahood.

It is said that following the bodhisattva path according to the Sutrayana, the common path as opposed to the uncommon path of the Vajrayana, requires three countless eons or even longer! From the moment that you have become a bodhisattva, your mind is bodhichitta, which arises spontaneously as a constant flow. You accumulate merit whatever you are doing. It takes one countless eon to get from there—the path of accumulation—to the first bodhisattva stage, corresponding to the path of seeing. Then it takes a second countless eon to get from the first to the eighth bodhisattva stage. From the eighth stage, moving through the ninth and tenth to its culmination, buddhahood, takes another countless eon. It might even require seven, according to His Holiness the Dalai Lama. These vast time frames demonstrate how very difficult it is to eradicate our subtlest obscurations. Yet the *Vajra Essence* tells us how to accomplish all of that in one lifetime. This direct path is the central theme of our text.

Each of the paths of the shravakas, pratyekabuddhas, and bodhisattvas has its own distinct characteristics, and they culminate in different degrees of realization. The shravakas see that everything that appears as a self, which is the basis of grasping on to "I" and "mine," is devoid of inherent nature. The pratyekabuddhas realize all outer and inner phenomena as dependently related illusory appearances. For bodhisattvas the power of realizing emptiness arises in the nature of compassion, effortlessly subsuming all aspects of skillful means and wisdom. All such realizations gained along the developmental paths of the shravakas, pratyekabuddhas, and bodhisattvas are subsumed by the path of discovery of the Great Perfection. Nonetheless, since achieving shamatha is a prerequisite to the fully effective practice of vipashyana, everyone—whether in the Theravada, Mahayana, or Vajrayana—has to pass through the nine stages of attentional development preceding the achievement of shamatha. Nobody bypasses them. Likewise, whether you are following the Sutrayana or Vajrayana, you must traverse those five paths. You might do so very swiftly, but there's no way to buddhahood apart from the five paths and ten bodhisattva stages.

Dzogchen of course, differs from the other schools. When I view it within the broader context of Buddhadharma, however, it appears to me to have an all-encompassing quality to it—it subsumes all of the other teachings I have ever heard in Buddhism. It has a place for them and embraces them. In fact there is a variant of the translation of the term *Dzogchen* (a condensation of *dzogpa chenpo*, normally rendered as "Great Perfection"), and that is "Great Encompassment." *Dzogpa* can mean something that "includes," "enfolds," is "complete." So the Great Perfection encompasses all of these other traditions.

> "This [the swift path of the clear light Great Perfection] is the most sublime of all dharmas. It is a general synthesis of all the paths, the goal of all spiritual vehicles, and an expansive treasury of all secret mantras. Only those that have stored vast collections of merit in many ways, over incalculable eons, will encounter this path. They will have aspired repeatedly and extensively to reach the state of perfect enlightenment, and they will have previously sought the path through other vehicles, establishing propensities to reach this path. No others will encounter it.
>
> "Why not? Although people lacking such fortune may be present where this vehicle is being explained and heard, because they are under the influence of their negative deeds and the strength of the powerful, devious maras of mental afflictions, their minds will be in a wilderness 2,500 miles away. Such unfortunate servants of maras with their perverse aspirations act contrary to this profound Dharma and respond to it with abuse, false conjecture, repudiation, envy, and so on.

Although we hope that all sentient beings, sooner or later, will progress along these stages and paths of liberation, the passage above says something to you, the reader, about your own circumstances. You should take these words personally. People who have encountered this path "will have aspired repeatedly and extensively to reach the state of perfect enlightenment, and they will have previously sought the path through other vehicles, establishing propensities"—karmic momentum—"to reach this path. No others will encounter it."

The reason others won't encounter this path is due to *maras*, a metaphor for mental afflictions. These do devilish work on us, they torment us. Because they are still under the domination of these mental afflictions, even though such people may be physically present when such teachings are given, "their minds will be in a wilderness 2,500 miles away." They are present at the teachings in the flesh but not in spirit—like a toddler present at one of physicist Stephen Hawking's lectures on quantum mechanics at Cambridge. In no meaningful sense can that child participate in that lecture.

As another example I recall a sermon I once heard from a Christian pastor. He raised the question: "How is it that people will enter into a religious tradition and after a while they just wander off and lose it?" He gave the analogy of a flock of five hundred sheep. How could one of these sheep get lost when it has 499 comrades all going, "baa, baa"? After all, this amounts to a chorus blaring out, "Here we are!" The answer is: "blade by blade." As for lost sheep, so for people in the Dharma, until after a while they just don't have any Dharma any more. How did they get lost? Well, there was this really cool video game...then this really good movie came on...then their friends wanted to go out for a beer and they said, "Why not?"...and then they lost their job—that was a big blade...and then they got a new job...and then there was this really interesting relationship they got into...and then, and then...and then their life is over.

Now the question naturally arises, "Am I like the toddler or the lost sheep—or am I one of those fortunate beings?" The answer is not so mysterious. From your own experience you will know whether your mind is 2,500 miles away or whether you really have the fortune to be present at and to receive teachings of this sort.

Observe the mind and it becomes clear that when you are dominated by mental afflictions, you are indeed a servant of maras. No one ever voluntarily decides to do so—to simply fly into a rage, become caught up in craving, to suddenly out of a blue sky become jealous. It always happens involuntarily, which means you are in servitude. The mental affliction arises; it captures us and imprisons us. Dharma exists to free us from that kind of bondage. The "perverse aspirations" of those who serve maras resonates with Shantideva's statement, in his *Guide to the Bodhisattva Way of Life*, that "Those desiring to escape from suffering hasten right toward suffering. With the very desire for happiness, out of delusion they destroy their own happiness as if it were an enemy."[9]

"On the other hand, those who enter the gateway of this Dharma and implement its meaning will appear as rarely as stars during the daytime. Some, when entering the path, will hear and understand a little, then abandon it and casually go astray. Not engaging in spiritual practice, they will face death as ordinary beings, and they will not achieve liberation.

In contrast to those people whose minds are 2,500 miles away, "those who enter the gateway of this Dharma," the "swift path of the clear light Great Perfection"—Dzogchen—"and implement its meaning," put it into practice, are as rare as stars during the daytime. For the record, it is true that stars may on rare occasions appear in the daytime as supernovas. This part of the text is reminiscent of the Biblical metaphor from Jesus, where he spoke of sowing seeds—some fell on dry ground, some on stone, and some in places they were able to fully germinate. "Some, when entering the path, will hear and understand a little, then abandon it and casually go astray," like a seed sown on very thin soil, which germinates but then dies.

QUALIFICATIONS OF A STUDENT OF THE GREAT PERFECTION

"In general, to enter this vehicle and put it into practice, you must have all of the following characteristics:
- belief in the Dharma and in your guru
- unwavering trust in the path
- earnest mindfulness of death and the conviction that all composite phenomena are impermanent, so that you have little attraction to mundane activities
- contentment with respect to food, wealth, and enjoyments
- insatiability for Dharma due to a great zeal and determination
- integration of life and spiritual practice, without complaining

By distinguishing those things to be taken literally from that which is provisional, we discover the core themes of the Dharma. These emerge quite clearly in this text. These themes include bodhichitta, the realization of emptiness, buddha nature, and the possibility of overcoming mental afflictions. From another angle, we can observe the broad framework of Dharma based on such things as ethics, samadhi,[10] wisdom, and the six perfections.

Regarding "belief in the Dharma," there is a danger that overemphasizing faith alone may lead to spiritual sloth. I have seen this occur in both Western students and in Tibetans. One pitfall is the spiritual sloth of self-effacement. There are Tibetans who are very strong when it comes to belief in the Dharma but who take the attitude: "I am not a tulku, so why should I meditate? Meditation is for great beings, not an ordinary person like me." That is the downside of the marvelous hagiographies of great beings such as Milarepa, Tsongkhapa, Jigmé Lingpa, and Düdjom Lingpa. They can inspire, but they can also be intimidating.

In order to avoid the notion of *faith*, it may be more useful to think of the approach of the *working hypothesis*. In other words, we may provisionally adopt certain views and live in accordance with them while at the same time doing our best to put them to the test of experience so that we can discover for ourselves whether they are true. We can use the hypotheses that shamatha was designed for people like us; ethics was designed for us; bodhichitta was something to be cultivated by people like us. We hypothesize that these are all things we can accomplish. According to His Holiness the Dalai Lama, if we practice like the great beings of the past, we will have the same realizations.

This then is a pragmatic approach to belief. We start from where we are rather than engaging in wishful thinking, embroidering, and speculation. We are not taking the attitude that simply because we believe something, this guarantees some outcome, such as our being "saved" or our going to some pleasant destination after death. Rather, we must be willing to reassess our beliefs as we go along, keeping an open mind. So when someone says, "Padmasambhava is here, now," what does that really mean? If you believe you have buddha nature, what does that mean? What does it mean to believe that there is continuity of consciousness from lifetime to lifetime? The hypothesis must be explored, tested. For instance, you may have had for some time the belief that karmic imprints carry over from lifetime to lifetime. But on reassessing that old hypothesis you may discover that this is a rather crude formulation in comparison to new and subtler knowledge you have acquired. So you revisit and reassess such hypotheses from time to time, giving them greater meaning. The basis for this approach is to keep an open mind, which is what we've been asked to do from the very beginning.

What about "belief...in your guru"? Here again we can use a working hypothesis. The teacher needn't be a bodhisattva, but he or she should have an altruistic motivation and a sound understanding of the subject matter. We can waste a lot of time wondering, "Has lama X or teacher Y achieved A?" Keeping in mind that lamas, teachers, and serious students of Dharma are always in flux, trying to pin down their realizations is pointless. It is more important for us to have faith in Samantabhadra, in Padmasambhava, in the Buddha. These are not merely historical figures; they are here with us right now. The qualities necessary for us to receive teachings from Padmasambhava are the openness of our hearts, our receptivity when listening, and faith in the presence of Padmasambhava. Then, if Padmasambhava or Buddha Shakyamuni is our true guru, any qualified teacher can bring to us their blessings and wisdom. Therefore, check the teacher's qualifications and motivation. Ask yourself if the teacher has knowledge you don't have or has had realization that you have not yet attained. Of course, if you don't have confidence that the teacher's motivation is altruistic, then you should find another teacher.

In addition to the two basic qualities a teacher must possess—altruistic intention and a sound knowledge of Dharma—three qualities are necessary on the part of a disciple. The first is perceptivity—attending closely, clarity of attention. "What is taking place in my mind, my speech, in other people's speech? Am I picking up what's going on?" A student who is not perceptive is not a suitable disciple and is not going to achieve enlightenment. The second quality is having an aspiration to put the teachings into practice. You aren't receiving teachings merely to accumulate knowledge, or because the lama is charismatic, your friends are going, or other reasons. You have come because you really want to practice. Otherwise you are wasting the teacher's time, which is a grave thing to do. The third quality is to attend to the teachings without prejudice, especially the prejudice of uncritically believing that your own ideas are true, while any assertion that differs from your beliefs is suspect. In other words, it's imperative to have an open mind, one willing to critically reassess even your own most cherished assumptions. These three qualities, like those necessary in a teacher, are crucial.

To enter this path, this vehicle, this "swift path of the clear light Great Perfection," not only do you need just those qualities, you must hone them, sharpen them. Then take this one step further: Since Düdjom Lingpa is saying that if you have these qualities you are suitable to follow this path, adopt the self-assurance that you are truly a suitable vessel for these teachings. Next go through them and see if you have some weak points, areas that could be improved. Burnish them and then return to that assurance: These are teachings for me. These are teachings that I could practice, that I could follow, just as the great Dzogchen masters of the past have done.

What is "earnest mindfulness of death," and what is its value? This virtue is put into practice by living with death in the back of your mind, and sometimes in the front of your mind, and becoming very comfortable with it. This recognition puts things into sharp focus—gives us "the conviction that all composite phenomena are impermanent, so that you have little attraction to mundane activities." In light of our death, our mundane desires are seen for what they are. For example: I feel a desire for my favorite bread, and then I get some and eat it. In normal, conventional circumstances that may be meaningful. In the face of death, it is completely irrelevant. How much sourdough bread I have eaten in this lifetime won't be something I care about when I am dying. From that perspective all the mundane concerns are likewise valueless. If our desires for wealth, luxury, good food, praise, reputation, affection, acceptance by other people, and so forth are worth nothing in the face of death, then that is precisely their ultimate value. Furthermore, anything unwholesome we've done in the pursuit of mundane concerns is going to have a negative impact. Maintain that perspective.

There is, however, another side to that coin. Just as we can overindulge in the mundane concerns, we can also go to the other extreme by overindulging in austerity. If we set inordinately high ascetic goals for our practice we can create obstacles and even injure ourselves physically and mentally.

In fact, creature comforts can be an aid to practice. It is good to have a comfortable home where you feel at ease, where your mind is spacious, where you can settle down and practice Dharma. If you need to get from here to there, what is wrong with having a dependable automobile? Luxuries may also have their place. At times you become tired and need a break—some entertainment, listening to a little music—why not? The same goes for the enjoyments of friendship, nature, and sex as well. Unless you have taken a monk's vows, there is nothing wrong with that. There can be no denying the beauty of intimacy, the warmth and love that can be shared in that context. Getting hung up on how much sex you are having is an overindulgence, but if sex forms part of the intimacy of a loving relationship, especially a Dharma relationship, there's nothing wrong with it.

In the same vein, we needn't become overly concerned about praise. If praise were entirely bad, then we should never praise each other or acknowledge someone's good qualities and actions because that would be feeding them poison. On the contrary, praise can be very helpful—receiving the acknowledgment, the affection, the acceptance, the respect of those around us. Mundane concerns have a place as long as our central motivation is the practice of Dharma. It is only when we invert things—when for instance we practice Dharma so people will like us more or to improve our material situation—that we devalue our practice and make a mockery of Dharma.

Still, the earnest mindfulness of death puts everything into perspective. It sets our priorities straight, which is what Dharma boils down to. Awareness of death helps us to recognize that everything to which we cling—including teachers, icons, altars, texts, traditions, teachings, Dharma settings, the time we put in on our cushion, let alone all of our mundane concerns—all of that is subject to impermanence. It all passes. Therefore, "all composite phenomena are impermanent . . . you have little attraction to mundane activities." He doesn't say *no* attraction. He says "little attraction." So, when I reach out for the plate of sourdough bread and it falls on the floor, I won't be terribly perturbed.

"Contentment with respect to food, wealth, and enjoyments": The monastic ideal is to be content with that which is adequate. So contentment on the one hand with regard to the food—the food is "good enough," the wealth—"got enough." And as for enjoyments: again it's nice to have some diversion once in a while, perhaps a walk or some music occasionally. So on the one hand you have contentment with regard to the mundane, but "insatiability"—just the opposite of contentment—for Dharma. With great zeal and determination, you just cannot get enough of Dharma. Until you are enlightened you are insatiable.

Finally we come to "integration of life and spiritual practice, without complaining": You want to have total integration. For instance, if you are alternating a week of retreat with three weeks living in your normal situation, then you would spend a week on nothing other than concerted focus on specific formal practices followed by thorough integration of them into your life in the following weeks. You continue on in that manner, dipping back in maybe a bit deeper in formal practice and then once more effecting thorough integration in daily life. The idea of course is that your practice and your life are coextensive. Like oil seeping into paper, there is no part of the paper that is not touched by the oil. And whatever life dishes up for you in terms of difficulties and challenges, you meet them with composure, without complaining.

There are only six points, as listed above. None of them are daunting, none are intimidating; nor are they impossible. In all of them there is the opportunity for greater growth, deeper conviction in Dharma, deeper trust in the guru, deeper trust in the path, a clearer, more vigilant, crisp awareness of death, greater contentment. Basically there is a growing insatiability for Dharma. Why? Because you love it so much. That's what zeal is. It's not just love, there is also that steel behind it—knowing that the practice of Dharma won't always be fun. That's where determination comes in. This is like driving along in fourth gear and then suddenly you're in potholes going up a steep incline. That's the time to downshift back into second. Second gear is determination. You just get through it with sheer determination and faith that Dharma is meaningful. Sooner or later things smooth out and zeal returns. You're not always going to be practicing joyfully; it just doesn't work that way. Still the bottom line is that you keep returning to joyous zeal as your ground state.

Sentient beings suffer in myriad ways. We suffer depression, anxiety, misery, grief, despair. On the path of Dharma that suffering can be magnificently meaningful. Instead of weaving your way around all the potholes of life, you take all the suffering that may come your way—some of it even catalyzed by your Dharma practice—and you transmute it into Dharma practice. So even in the midst of suffering, even when misery or conflict or internal strife or mental afflictions seem to dominate your mind—filling the space of the mind, capturing you, enslaving you—even then *your mind is larger* than all that. I love that phrase and find it very meaningful. The space of your awareness is larger than the space of your convoluted mind. That doesn't mean the mind isn't afflicted. You are just seeing it from a wider angle, where some voice in you can say, "Oh, I see, my mind's afflicted; oh, I see, this is grief; this is despair," and so on.

This has happened to me on a number of occasions. I would have some hours of depression now and then when I was in retreat. I wondered how long it could last. I would sit down and watch it, and see "That was depression. Now it's getting less." As soon as it would get less, it would get less very quickly. Sometimes it would be as big as a rhinoceros. It filled up a lot of my mind, but never all of it. So I would say, "Ah, that's depression." Or "Ah, that's elation." Or "Ah, that's hope; ah, that's fear." In addition there was one big bogeyman that I got to recognize very well: "How fast am I progressing?" That's the spiritual version of "Are we there yet, Daddy?" "How fast am I progressing? Am I moving?" is one of the most pernicious impediments. So I would look at that one and just smile.

DIFFICULTIES INHERENT IN OTHER VEHICLES

"When such people with stable minds—without being boastful about the mere number of months or years they have spent practicing in retreat—see this entrance and undertake the practice, they will definitely achieve the supreme state of Buddha Vajradhara in this very lifetime. In other vehicles, it is said that after collecting the accu-

mulations and purifying obscurations for three countless eons, finally
you become perfectly enlightened. Nevertheless, because of karma,
mental afflictions, and habitual propensities gathered over eons,
through the course of many lifetimes, the influences of various
thoughts and actions make it difficult to encounter the path of accumulation and purification. Think carefully about this situation, and
you will become clear and certain of it.

Bear in mind that when Düdjom Lingpa states that those with stable minds
who enter and undertake this practice "will definitely achieve the supreme
state of Buddha Vajradhara in this very lifetime," thirteen of his disciples
actually did that, which is awesome.

In other vehicles such as the Shravakayana, Pratyekabuddhayana, and
so forth, there are two types of accumulations that may be collected. There
is the accumulation of merit, relating to *upaya*, skillful means—skillful methods of generosity, ethics, patience, enthusiasm, and even samadhi. Then
there is the accumulation of knowledge, which culminates in the realization
of the dharmakaya, omniscience. The accumulation of merit finally leads to
the realization of the form bodies—the nirmanakaya and sambhogakaya—
of a buddha.

Purification refers specifically to cleansing obscurations resulting from
negative acts performed in the past and of the obscurations of the mental
afflictions. The great difficulty lies in the powerful momentum of our karma,
and sheer habit. The deep ruts of our habitual thinking and behavior have
been accumulated over many eons of previous lives. So in the Mahayana
tradition you practice the six perfections for three countless eons until
finally you become perfectly enlightened—a buddha—with the thirty-two
major and eighty minor marks. That's how long it takes, though—three
countless eons. It's finite, but don't hold your breath. You are practicing
through contractions and expansions of the universe—basically big bangs
and big crunches.

Consider the wide array of karma we've accumulated in the past. Even in
this lifetime—if you've been here for a while—you may have done something pretty nasty on occasion. How do we know when that particular

karma will catalyze and throw us somewhere we don't particularly want to go? We can purify, but as long as we are prone to mental afflictions, how do we know when the next one's going to appear, not to mention habitual propensities—the sheer habit of samsara? We simply don't know. Because of these nasty actions and afflicted mental states, "gathered over eons, through the course of many lifetimes, the influences of various thoughts and actions make it difficult to encounter the path of accumulation and purification." Can I have total confidence that in each succeeding lifetime I will meet qualified teachers, conducive environments, that I'll always have the aspiration to practice and always devote myself to practice? Dubious.

Therefore, since it is difficult for us to encounter, and progress well along, the path of accumulation and purification, the Teacher advises us to "think carefully about this situation, and you will become clear and certain of it."

> "Be that as it may, due to excellent karmic connections from the past, now you have obtained a sublime human life with freedom and opportunity, and you have encountered the most sublime of dharmas, the secret mantra, Vajrayana. This is no time to hold on to the hope of accumulating merit over a long period until you finally attain enlightenment.

Once we have obtained a human life of leisure and opportunity, and within that we have encountered a living tradition of Vajrayana, and specifically, Dzogchen—relatively swift paths—it makes little sense to opt for accumulating wisdom and merit over an immensely long time in order to achieve enlightenment. The Teacher is saying that we should banish the thought of taking such a slow, gradual path to enlightenment—forget about it. Rather, focus on the circumstances and opportunities we have right now, and don't take them for granted. Doing so would be like encountering a wish-fulfilling jewel—a metaphor from ancient Buddhist lore for an extremely valuable object that is incredibly difficult to find—and then throwing it over your shoulder, saying, "I'll find another one later."

"Rather, you must apprehend the ground of your own being for yourself, by experiencing the intrinsic nature of the sugatagarbha, the primordial ground that is the path to liberation in this lifetime.

I think I can be happily dogmatic on this point: there is only one path to achieve enlightenment in one lifetime, and that is by realizing your own self-nature. This won't happen simply by being enormously generous or ethical or patient. All of those are great, but to achieve enlightenment in this lifetime, there is no way other than to realize the depths of your own identity, the depths of your own nature—your buddha nature.

In Dzogchen, as well as in other Buddhist traditions, you find teachings on the ground, path, and fruition. The ground is your starting point—the nature of existence as it is. The path is the trajectory you follow to the goal, enlightenment. The fruition is the fulfillment—the enlightenment that you seek. Characteristically, Vajrayana takes the fruition itself as the path. Before we manifest and experience the qualities of an enlightened being such as Padmasambhava, we do our best to assume that identity, to take on that role. We are rehearsing to become Padmasambhava—getting used to it. This is our birthright anyway, so we slip into those shoes even before we can really fill them. This approach—taking the fruition as the path—saves us countless eons.

The ground can be viewed from several perspectives. The relative ground is the reality we typically see appearing before us, the ocean of samsara, where we're bound and manacled in that iron cage—blind, hurtling down the river of rebirth. This pathetic situation is where we're starting from, and it's the reason we take refuge. We are both helpless and pretty hopeless all by ourselves. There's a lot of suffering here, and our minds are very prone to mental afflictions. Even when resting, mental afflictions appear. There is another ground beneath that ground, however—an ultimate ground. In Dzogchen that deeper ground is taken as the path. Here your ground is the sugatagarbha, buddha nature. It's not some future enlightenment, some future fruition. You take it now—take the future fruition and bring it to the path. You take the deepest ground, which is already present, and in so doing you discover that the ground, the path, and the fruition are all of one taste.

If you are seeking liberation and awakening in this lifetime, then this is the way to proceed. As long as you sustain the notion of your ordinary self, your ordinary identity, and think all you have is a *potential* for enlightenment that you'll be able to manifest if you are really good for a really long time; and as long as you're looking upon your guru as an ordinary person—as long as you are locked into those reified notions of ordinary appearances— then you might as well get out your stopwatch and begin counting off three countless eons plus all the time it takes you to become a bodhisattva. It will not be a short path. On the other hand, if you would like to speed things up a bit, you'll have to break some old habits—for example, who you think you are.

> "Apart from this, the teachings that the state of liberation results from accumulating much karma from one life to another are effective for bringing about temporary happiness in the minds of beings, but enlightenment in this way is extremely difficult. Consider that such teachings may have a merely provisional meaning."

As we saw earlier, it is improbable that you will be able to marshal all of your future lifetimes like ducks in a row, where each one provides all of the circumstances necessary to continue on the path. That's extremely difficult, considering the hodgepodge of karma, mental afflictions, and habitual propensities accumulated in the past. If the texture of our lives up to now has been such a mishmash, it is difficult to imagine having uniformity in the future.

At this point the Teacher provides a very provocative conclusion— suggesting that we consider that those teachings—the Sutrayana, the long path—"may have a merely provisional meaning." In other words, maybe they were never meant to be taken literally. He didn't specifically say they are not to be taken literally, but he did say, "think it over."

> Bodhisattva Great Boundless Emptiness commented, "O Teacher, Bhagavan, you can achieve liberation by striving in this present human life for good thoughts that expand the mind and for bodily

and verbal virtues, and then, at some future time, by practicing the view and meditation of the clear light Great Perfection, the vajra essence of secret mantra. But it is said that it is difficult to achieve liberation through this life's practice alone. Moreover, it is said that small-minded beings, such as shravakas and pratyekabuddhas, cannot fathom the vast and profound Vajrayana Dharma. Is this true or not? If it is true, and the quality and capacity of the minds of beings differs, then the small-minded would have to expand their minds to become beings of the Mahayana class, and some beings would not be able to expand their minds sufficiently. If this were so, they would have to acquire some secret mantra from somewhere other than their own mindstream. If this were the case, I don't know what it would mean. Teacher, please explain!"

The bodhisattva begins by laying out one track we could take, one possibility: Since it is so difficult to achieve enlightenment in one lifetime, why don't we just apply ourselves to conventional virtue—the six perfections and so forth—and then some lifetime when we're more mature, we can get around to Dzogchen? Then he speaks of another track, that of "small-minded beings, such as shravakas and pratyekabuddhas," who "cannot fathom the vast and profound Vajrayana Dharma," who are striving solely for their own liberation; they just want a one-way ticket out of samsara, "every man for himself"—which of course is a small-minded attitude and unsuitable for even comprehending a faster path.

Next Bodhisattva Great Boundless Emptiness speculates that to be a truly suitable vessel for Dzogchen you would need an incredibly vast mind. Those without such a mind would seemingly have to evolve into a new species. That is, starting out small-minded, they would have to go through some process of transmutation to become "big-minded," as in Mahayana, and then expand even more to have a mind vast enough for Dzogchen. "If this were so, they would have to acquire some secret mantra," that is to say Vajrayana, "from somewhere other than their own mindstream." Those with small- or medium-sized minds would need to acquire knowledge from outside to meet the standard apparently required of a student of Dzogchen. To encapsulate, he is saying: "From what I hear, this seems to be the case. But if it's true, it doesn't make sense to me. Teacher, please explain!"

THE TIME TO PRACTICE VAJRAYANA

He replied, "O Great Boundless Emptiness, in this present lifetime, if you arrive with that question at the gateway of secret mantra—and you have firm faith and belief, and strong, unflagging enthusiasm— the time has come to practice. When fortunate beings come to the gateway of the profound secret mantra, apart from simply having strong faith and belief, there is never anything else—such as clair- voyance, omens, or auspicious circumstances—to make them think that the time has come to practice secret mantra. Once you have obtained a human life and encountered a guru and the secret mantra Dharma, if this is not the time to practice the Great Per- fection, then there will never be a better time than this in another life—this is certain.

The Teacher replies by saying, in essence: "You have recognized the prob- lem, you have fathomed the contradiction. Good. Now, if you have faith in Dzogchen, if you are truly ready to commit yourself to practice, your question itself indicates to me the time is ripe, that you are indeed ready to actually practice Dzogchen." The Teacher then elaborates that "apart from simply having strong faith and belief," not blind, dogmatic faith, but will- ingness to be guided by a working hypothesis, "there is never anything else," such as clairvoyance or omens, to help you decide. You know that you have no absolute proof, but you are willing to launch your spiritual practice based on this premise. That's a belief that has power; that's accepting a working hypothesis that radically transforms your life.

Great Boundless Emptiness has posed a most reasonable question. Hav- ing encountered such awesome teachings, the depth of which is incon- ceivable, you could easily wonder, "Am I up to this?" Unless you were possessed of sheer arrogance, thinking that you are far superior to others, how would you have the confidence, the chutzpah, to say, "I am a suitable vessel for these teachings?" The Teacher has answered, saying: Number one, you have encountered them. Your karma has brought you here. Karma is enough to get you to the gateway. Number two, faith is enough to get you through that door. If those two are there, he tells us, have no more qualms. Don't wait for some special auspicious sign or for a lama to say that you are a chosen disciple. If you have faith, enthusiasm, love for the practice, that's all you need. It just doesn't get any better than this.

> "It is not that the minds of shravakas, pratyekabuddhas, ordinary beings, and so forth are too small. Rather, due to their previous karma, they do not reach the gateway of the secret mantra. Or even if they do, they have no faith and no belief, and because of spiritual sloth and distraction, they don't practice.

Now we are given a clearer picture as to why some are suitable vessels for Dzogchen and others are not. The "small-minded versus big-minded" argument makes no sense because that isn't the crux of the matter. It is "rather, due to their previous karma" that most people don't reach the gateway of the secret mantra—they simply don't encounter it. It is not a matter of their being small-minded. Their karma has not evolved to the point where they are ready to encounter that gateway. "Or even if they do"—perhaps due to some favorable karma they stumble upon a book or wander into a teaching—and even if they receive a favorable impression, thinking, "These are some really cool mystical teachings," they put off doing practice, and it comes to nothing.

BODHICHITTA

> "Understand that this has nothing to do with the specific capacities of beings' minds. Don't think that there are any differences in the capacities of the minds of beings. To those fettered by selfishness, I teach that by opening their hearts to all beings throughout space, without concern for their own welfare, they will see the truth of the nonduality of self and other."

Now we are going to the heart of the matter, bodhichitta—the gateway between the so-called small-minded—the shravakas and pratyekabuddhas— as opposed to the so-called large-minded of the "great vehicle," the Mahayana, for which bodhichitta is the core. The Teacher isn't saying that people have different capacities *per se*. Rather he is saying that your past karma brings you to that point in your spiritual evolution where you not only encounter but *wish to immerse yourself* in Dzogchen. At this point the text turns to the topic of bodhichitta.

> Great Boundless Emptiness continued, "O Teacher, Bhagavan, if so, is it impossible for them to expand their minds by meditating on the profound mystery of the Great Perfection? Or, even if they meditate on the Great Perfection, do they need to develop the spirit of awakening in some other way? Teacher, please explain!"

Great Boundless Emptiness is asking about those beings that are prone to self-centeredness, who are not yet bodhisattvas. This returns us to the question, "How mature do we need to be in order to be able to practice Dzogchen effectively?" Or, in other words, "Do you need to be a bodhisattva to do so?" So, for beings like ourselves who are still fettered, still encumbered by self-centeredness, taking our own well-being as more important than anybody else's, is it impossible for us to expand our minds by meditating on the Great Perfection? And even if we meditate in such a way, do we need to develop the spirit of awakening in some other way apart from the practice of the Great Perfection? Must we become a bodhisattva first, and then venture into Dzogchen? Or can we go for Dzogchen but make sure we cultivate bodhichitta as well? That's the question.

> He replied, "O noble one, this Great Perfection is the vehicle of the unsurpassed fruition. That which manifests the great reality that pervades all samsara and nirvana is called the spirit of awakening of the ultimate ground; you need apprehend only this. Apart from this, intellectually fabricating with effort a so-called 'spirit of awakening' entails generating a mental state in which you view yourself as the

meditator and other sentient beings as objects of meditation—an
attitude that is as limited as a teacup.

Practicing the Great Perfection, "the vehicle of the unsurpassed fruition,"
means that you make the fruition—buddhahood—the vehicle by which
you attain buddhahood. This, as mentioned previously, is "taking the
fruition as the path." "The spirit of awakening of the ultimate ground" is also
translated as "ultimate bodhichitta." In this context, ultimate bodhichitta is
dharmakaya, rigpa, or primordial consciousness.

In the Gelug tradition, too, they speak of both relative and ultimate
bodhichitta. There, relative bodhichitta is the heartfelt aspiration to achieve
enlightenment for the benefit of all beings. That falls within the Sutrayana.
Ultimate bodhichitta, again within the Sutrayana, is the unmediated, nondual, nonconceptual realization of emptiness. In the context of Dzogchen,
relative bodhichitta is the same as it is defined by the Gelugpa. Ultimate
bodhichitta, on the other hand, is rigpa, pristine awareness, rather than
emptiness as presented in the Sutrayana. So once again we have a balance—
ultimate and relative, two truths, not just one; and yet the two truths are of
the same nature. According to the *Vajra Essence* you need only apprehend
"the spirit of awakening of the ultimate ground." This is in response to the
question about self-centeredness and developing bodhichitta. All you need
to apprehend is your own buddha nature. That will suffice.

Within the Sutrayana context of relative bodhichitta and ultimate
bodhichitta, the two are sequential. First there's relative bodhichitta
accomplished with effort. You strive diligently to overcome strong habitual propensities. For example, there's one candy bar on the table and someone is reaching for it, but I am quicker and grab it first. That's the
manifestation of an old habit: "If somebody's going to get something good,
it should be me. If someone is going to get something bad, it shouldn't be
me." To overcome that deep current of sheer irascible habit takes a lot of
effort. Shantideva in *A Guide to the Bodhisattva Way of Life* tells us how. Practicing bodhichitta with effort, you strive to overcome self-centeredness.
You practice *tonglen*, practice loving-kindness, compassion, empathetic joy,
and equanimity. You must overcome the tremendous momentum of "me

first," which is difficult. Then some facsimile of bodhichitta arises, and you can genuinely say, "I truly wish to achieve enlightenment for the benefit of all beings." You get there the hard way, by sheer effort to overcome the old propensities, your selfishness. That is bodhichitta with effort; that is relative bodhichitta.

Using such a developmental model, eventually the tide turns and bodhichitta arises more and more naturally, spontaneously, and effortlessly. Gradually your predilections, your habits for self-centeredness, subside. At that point seeing any sentient being suffering will catalyze bodhichitta, and you have become a bodhisattva. Although this form of bodhichitta is great, it is still dualistic. *Here* am I, the meditator, the bodhisattva. *Over there* is the sentient being who is the object of my compassion. In contrast to this dualistic attitude, which the Teacher calls "as limited as a teacup," is the ocean of direct realization of your buddha nature. An ocean cannot flow out of a teacup.

The Teacher states that all you need in order to overcome self-centeredness is to apprehend the spirit of awakening of the ultimate ground. That is all that's required for relative bodhichitta to emerge. Relative bodhichitta will flow from ultimate bodhichitta. This is one difference between the Sutrayana and Dzogchen. Within the Sutrayana, if you gain an unmediated realization of emptiness, this does not necessarily imply that you realize bodhichitta. Bodhichitta is needed as a complement to that realization. Wisdom and compassion need to be balanced. However, in Dzogchen, ultimate bodhichitta is not simply the realization of emptiness. It is the realization of primordial consciousness. If you have an unmediated realization of buddha nature, he says, that naturally yields the realization of relative bodhichitta. So keep in mind that realization of emptiness is not the same as realization of buddha nature, primordial consciousness. Comparing the two kinds of bodhichitta, the effortful, striving, struggling way is "as limited as a teacup." It is worth doing, because having a little teacup full of water is a lot better than dying of thirst in a desert of self-centeredness. But it is much better to have an ocean of compassion.

"In the expanse of the Great Perfection—the original nature of the great equality of samsara and nirvana—the mode of existence of the

ground itself is known just as it is by means of great, omniscient primordial consciousness. To speak of having a spirit of awakening greater than the vision of great, all-seeing primordial consciousness would be like saying you must seek liquid elsewhere, even though you already have water.

"The primordial, originally pure ground, the great reality that pervades the whole of samsara and nirvana, is the spirit of awakening. Without knowing this, even the benign sense of love and compassion that parents have for their children is a conceptual, object-focused state of mind. With that alone, you might aspire for a fortunate rebirth; but hoping it will lead to enlightenment is as senseless as hoping that the son of a barren woman will become a householder."

"The mode of existence of the ground itself is known just as it is by means of great, omniscient primordial consciousness." That is to say, the Great Perfection is known by nondual realization. Within the Dzogchen context, relative bodhichitta is utterly subsumed by ultimate bodhichitta. Therefore, even if you venture into Dzogchen without being a bodhisattva, while still having some tendencies toward self-centeredness, you can bring what antidotes you have to the practice. By focusing skillfully on Dzogchen and then gaining realization, however, all of that self-centeredness will be swept away. Then relative bodhichitta will arise as a byproduct of your realization of rigpa.

To state that "the primordial, originally pure ground, the great reality that pervades the whole of samsara and nirvana, is the spirit of awakening" is to say that buddha nature *is* bodhichitta. He then describes the normal sense of love and compassion parents have for their children as a "conceptual, object-focused state of mind." This is an "I-you" relationship, and it is wonderful—immeasurably better than an "I-it" relationship, or engaging with others simply out of self-centeredness or craving or hostility.[11] Nevertheless, it is still a conceptual, object-focused state of mind. Hoping that this kind of love and compassion will lead to enlightenment "is as senseless as hoping that the son of a barren woman will become a householder"; it is hoping for the impossible. Relative bodhichitta will not by itself give rise to ultimate bodhichitta. It can be a tremendous aid, which is why all the lamas who teach Dzogchen also teach relative bodhichitta. They give teachings on Shantideva's *Guide to the Bodhisattva Way of Life*, the four thoughts that turn the mind toward Dharma, and the preliminary practices (*ngöndro*). These will all enhance, support, and nurture the practice of Dzogchen. The absolute doesn't arise from the relative, but if you penetrate through to the ultimate, the relative will arise from that.

4

TAKING THE MIND AS THE PATH

As a prelude to Bodhisattva Great Boundless Emptiness' next question to Samantabhadra, let's briefly review the teaching to this point. The request that initiated the whole conversation was "Please grant us the profound pith instructions to actually achieve the state of the fully perfected Buddha Samantabhadra, in one lifetime and with one body." After the dialogue flowing from that request, Bodhisattva Great Boundless Emptiness probed further in terms of context—the question of Dzogchen versus the more common Dharma practices of engaging in the wholesome and avoiding the unwholesome. Following the Teacher's response, the questions became still more specific and detailed, addressing the cultivation of bodhichitta from the Dzogchen perspective. So the text unfolds through a process of ever more subtle questioning of the Teacher. The questioner began with his primary motivation—the initial request—and then pursued derivative motivations in order to obtain a clearer and more detailed picture. Now the bodhisattva's next question refers back to his first question:

> Bodhisattva Great Boundless Emptiness requested, "O Teacher, Bhagavan, please teach us the profound path that liberates disciples!"
> He replied, "O noble one, entrances to the city of great liberation appear as many avenues of skillful means and wisdom. But ultimately, taking the mind as the path is the quest for the true way. Then, once you have determined the ground, you may take ultimate reality as

> the path. Between these two options, first, here is the way to take
> the mind as the path.

The Teacher begins by providing context: There is not just one path; there
are a multitude of paths. Whatever path you follow, however, if it bypasses
your mind, there is no way to reach the city of liberation. You must go
through your mind. The starting point is right here and right now. If I were
to ask you to look at your mind for one minute and then report, you could
tell me something, couldn't you? Using whatever abilities you have for
introspection, you observe, and what you perceive is the surface level of
your mind. You might say this is the gateway to your mind.

Your mind includes everything ranging from that which you can immediately introspect and report on all the way down to the very ground of the
ordinary mind. As Western psychologists such as Freud and Jung have recognized, most of the mind's activity is subconscious. When the teaching
says, "take the mind as your path," that means you make that which is subconscious conscious. You must point your laser beam right down through
the strata of your mind until you arrive at the ground of your mind. You cannot simply say, "Well, I know my mind is really messed up and that I'm neu-
rotic and kind of a jerk, but even so I'm just going to skip all that and
become a buddha." It doesn't work that way. You can't leave your "jerki-
ness" behind. You have to go through it, not around it. You can't just come
up with a lot of cool visualizations to pretend you're something you're not
and then think that you can skip your mind in the process.

Visualizations are fine. The stage of generation is important. Yet you
must still confront your mind; you have to go right through it. That is taking the mind as your path. You need to go to the very ground of the ordinary mind. This requires shamatha. You don't need vipashyana for that, nor
Dzogchen, nor bodhichitta. But you do need to go right to the ground of
your ordinary mind and let the mind settle, unforced. When the mind is
quiescent—no turbulent thoughts or emotions arising—it is relaxed, still,
luminous, and free from effort. That is shamatha.

"Then, once you have determined the ground," the relative ground, the
ground of the ordinary mind, that becomes your platform for realizing the

empty nature of your own mind—its lack of inherent nature—and the emptiness of all other phenomena as well, both subjective and objective—you "take ultimate reality as the path." Again, the Sanskrit term I translated as "ultimate reality" is *dharmata*. So once you have arrived at the ground of the ordinary mind, you are ready to break through the reified sense of your own mind by means of vipashyana—shattering that reified structure of awareness and then dropping to the ground, to the deepest level of ground awareness, primordial consciousness, your buddha nature. Having fathomed your buddha nature, that then becomes your path. Until you've fathomed your ultimate reality, your relative mind is the path.

The Buddha declared, "The wise one straightens the fluttering, unsteady mind, which is difficult to guard and hard to restrain, just as a fletcher straightens an arrow's shaft."[12] Likewise, he likened the mind to a lute that must be tuned perfectly—not too tight and not too slack. You tune your instrument until the pitch is perfect, and then you play; you practice vipashyana to realize the emptiness of inherent nature of all phenomena, and then you practice Dzogchen to realize rigpa. So the main question was, "What's the path that liberates us in one lifetime, so we become a buddha in one lifetime and with one body?" Right here we are given the answer: "Ultimately, taking the mind as the path is the quest for the true way. Then, once you have determined the ground," implying that you have ascertained your substrate consciousness by achieving shamatha, then you may take the ultimate reality of emptiness as the path. "Between these two options," of taking the mind as your path, which is shamatha, and taking ultimate reality as your path, which is vipashyana, first, "here is the way to take the mind as the path":

> "At the outset, disciples who maintain their samayas initially train their minds by way of the common, outer preliminaries—namely, the four thoughts that turn the mind—and the uncommon, seven inner preliminaries. Subsequently, the way to follow the progressive path of the main practice is like this: first, retreat to a secluded forest; pray to your guru; and merging your mind with your guru's, relax for a little while.

It is assumed that if you have received tantric *samayas*, or sacred pledges, you keep those commitments. The Teacher then refers to the four thoughts that turn the mind, which are the preciousness of a human life of leisure and opportunity, impermanence and death, the unsatisfying nature of samsaric existence, and karma. What is their importance? They help you align your priorities, orient you toward Dharma rather than toward mundane concerns, and place you on the path of Dharma. It is important throughout your spiritual life to attend to these four.

Although Düdjom Lingpa does not specify which seven inner preliminaries he is referring to, one such set includes (1) taking refuge and cultivating the spirit of awakening, (2) offering prostrations, (3) offering the mandala, (4) practicing the purificatory meditation and mantra of Vajrasattva, (5) guru yoga, (6) transference of consciousness (*phowa*), and (7) severance, or "cutting through" (*chö*).

I want to emphasize here that there is no one "right way" to perform the preliminaries, nor even one right format. Some traditions require that students do five sets of 100,000 prostrations, prayers for the cultivation of bodhichitta, recitations of the Vajrasattva mantra, mandala offerings, and guruyoga recitations before they begin Vajrayana practice—they simply are not allowed to receive Vajrayana teachings before they have completed those. In other traditions students begin those but then receive teachings and do Vajrayana practices intermittently. The esteemed Kalu Rinpoche said you can practice shamatha first and the preliminaries second, or you can complete the preliminaries first and then accomplish shamatha. In the Buddha's teachings recorded in the Pali canon and Sanskrit sutras, there are no references as far as I know to engaging in the above five sets of preliminary practices before venturing into shamatha. Since there is no single right way, it's important not to be dogmatic about assuming that everyone should practice as you do. What is important is that you find a way that is suitable for accumulating merit and dispelling obstacles. Bear in mind, you can accumulate merit not only by offering 100,000 mandalas or prostrations but also by being of service with your skills, your time, money, material goods, helping the less fortunate—all of that counts.

Generally speaking, practicing any kind of virtue is a purificatory act.

So let's not be rigid or mechanical. By practicing shamatha with a good motivation, you can also purify obscurations and accumulate a great deal of merit. The same goes for the four applications of mindfulness, the four immeasurables, dream yoga, Madhyamaka vipashyana, and, finally, Dzogchen. All of these purify.

Within Sutrayana, two practices have greater purifying power than any others. The first is bodhichitta. Shantideva, in the first chapter of *A Guide to the Bodhisattva Way of Life*, wrote, "Like the conflagration at the time of the destruction of the universe, bodhichitta consumes great vices in an instant."[13] The second great purifier is the realization of emptiness. The realization of emptiness overwhelms the mental afflictions. Any practice that facilitates bodhichitta or the realization of emptiness, such as taking refuge, *tonglen*, and the four thoughts that turn the mind, is greatly effective. The realization of emptiness and bodhichitta are, after all, the essence of wisdom and compassion—the two wings of enlightenment. Again, according to Shantideva, "From the time that you adopt bodhichitta with an irreversible attitude for the sake of liberating limitless sentient beings, from that moment on, an uninterrupted stream of merit, equal to the sky, constantly arises even when you are asleep or distracted."[14] Because of your motivation, merit accrues even when you are, for instance, just hanging out and watching television.

After keeping your sacred commitments, accumulating merit, turning your mind toward Dharma, and so on, the main practice is *taking the mind as the path*. There are many types of shamatha, not all of which take the mind as the path. However, the way to achieve shamatha described here is absolutely naked. There is no buffer zone of mantras, visualizations, or anything like that. "First, retreat to a secluded forest," and that could be a wilderness, the desert, or it could be your room. It must be a place where you can collect your mind, where you are undistracted, where you can be present and practice Dharma all the time. That is what is meant by "a secluded forest"—a place of seclusion, where you are completely focused. "Pray to your guru," pray for blessings, pray that your practice may flourish. Begin by visualizing your guru before you. This is an "I-Thou" relationship, which transcends the polarized distinction of self and other,

embracing both in a large, encompassing entirety. Offer prayers of supplication, and then once the prayers are done, imagine the guru coming to the
crown of your head, merging with yourself, being nondual with your body,
speech, and mind. "And merging your mind with your guru's, relax for a
little while."

THE PRIMACY OF MIND

"O Great Boundless Emptiness, among your body, speech, and mind,
which is most important? Which is the main agent? Tell me, which is
the unchanging, autonomous monarch? Then the acts of teaching
and listening and the nature of the instruction will become perfectly
clear, to the great benefit of disciples."

Here Samantabhadra turns the tables and questions Great Boundless
Emptiness. We wish to take the mind as the path, but what does that mean?
What is the mind? What is the referent of the word "mind"? Samantabhadra is asking for context regarding body, speech, and mind. Among
the three—body, speech, and mind—which is most important? Who is
responsible? Who is doing things? Which is the "unchanging, autonomous
monarch"?

In the kingdom of your body, speech, and mind—in the kingdom of
your life—do you not have a sense that someone is in charge? When you
are in your right mind—not ill, not delirious—someone is responsible,
someone is calling the shots, right? You woke up this morning, and that
"unchanging, autonomous monarch" seemed to be the same person who
woke up yesterday morning. Don't you sense that there seems to be something constant in the midst of all of the chaotic flux, the ebb and flow of
emotions, the proliferation of thoughts and moods that arise and vanish,
desires that come and go, the breath and sensations that rise and fall?
Don't you have a sense of there being something at the center that is
unchanging—something that is aware of it all, that is in charge of it, that
stands a bit apart, that is not just the stuff of the mind, not just the voice of
your thoughts, but maybe something that is directing the voice and likewise

the movements of your body? Who is that durable, constant, autonomous, standing-somewhat-apart "monarch"?

If the bodhisattva who already has a very profound understanding wishes to, he could say "I'm sorry Samantabhadra, but I've looked within and there is no such entity. I have absolutely no sense of there being an unchanging, autonomous monarch." But the Teacher assumes that we ordinary folk *do* have the perception that there is someone in charge. By investigating, by pursuing these questions among the body, speech, and mind, and preparing yourself to report back, "the acts of teaching and listening and the nature of the instruction will become perfectly clear, to the great benefit of disciples." Before we launch into the mind with shamatha, settling the mind in its natural state—thus taking the mind as the path—Samantabhadra asks that we pause and see whether we can clearly determine the actual nature of that which we are taking as our path.

> Bodhisattva Great Boundless Emptiness responded, "O Teacher, Bhagavan, the body is created by the mind. When matter and awareness separate at death, the mind follows after karma, and then it grasps on delusively to the appearance of a body once more. Moreover, your body in the waking state, your body while dreaming, and your bodies following this life are all created by the self-grasping mind. They are temporary transformations that have never existed except as mere appearances to the mind. Therefore, since the mind is the all-creating monarch, it is of the utmost importance.

Bodhisattva Great Boundless Emptiness rises to the challenge, responding that the body is created by the mind. If that is true, then in the modern West we've turned everything upside down. We believe that the mind is created by the body—the brain—and many people, including psychologists and neuroscientists, don't even pause to question that. Yet here the bodhisattva says the body is created by the mind.

How do you sense your body? Whether you use a microscope to observe at the genetic level or go up to the level of tissue, bone, and organs—everything that arises to you, all the knowledge you have of your body, consists of *appearances to your mind*. You never observe anything other than appearances to your mind, and I don't think there is a neurobiologist who challenges that. All our knowledge of matter derives from appearances to the mind. So in this sense, the body is created by the mind. It is this mind—which is formless, which has no shape, no color, and so forth—that gives rise to, for example, the appearances of the brain. When you touch an organ beneath your skin, you have tactile sensations, but they too are sensations arising to the mind. They are not some entity out there independent of the mind. If you touch your skin or any other part of your body, sensations of solidity, fluidity, warmth, and movement arise, corresponding to the four elements of earth, water, fire, and air. Everything you know about your body consists of appearances to the mind. This illustrates the meaning of the Buddha's statement, "All phenomena are preceded by the mind, issue forth from the mind, and consist of the mind."[15]

The metaphysical realist assumes that there's a real body out there that somehow corresponds in a one-to-one relationship with our mental images of the body. But the only thing we can really be sure that we know is awareness and appearances to awareness. Let's relate this to the distinction the Buddha made between "naming" (*nama*) and "appearance" (*rupa*). These may be regarded as two ways of looking at the one flow of conscious experience. Naming is experience seen subjectively as the mental process of identifying an object, while appearances are experiences seen objectively as entities that are perceived and conceived through the mental process of identification. Within this context, "mind" (*mano*) refers to the mental process of conceptualization, which integrates and makes meaning out of the different appearances that arise to the six senses. This meaningful total experience is viewed subjectively as the identification of an entity (*nama*) and objectively as the entity identified (*rupa*).[16]

"When matter and awareness separate at death, the mind follows after karma," and then you are coursing through the *bardo*, the intermediary state, experiencing the fruition of your karma, hastening after this and that. Then, as your bardo experience comes to an end, the mind "grasps on delusively to the appearance of a body once more." The flow of awareness conjoins with the body, mind emerges from the substrate consciousness, and the mind grasps on to appearances with the sense that "this is mine," as if there's something about the body that makes it intrinsically "mine." Once again we grasp on to "I" and "mine," with respect to the body and mind.

Some people look into the mirror and say, "that's me." Of course, what they are really seeing is an image created by their minds that they are taking to be a body and are grasping on to as themselves. Others are more sophisticated, saying—"That's a reflection of my body"—as if there's something really in the nature of the body itself that makes it mine. Likewise, "When matter and awareness separate at death, the mind follows after karma, and then it grasps on delusively to the appearance of a body once more."

"Moreover, your body in the waking state": Consider how many bodies you have over the course of a life and a death, for instance, "your body while dreaming." Last night I had numerous dreams, so in a sense I had multiple incarnations. I didn't have just one body; I had a whole bunch in just one night. You have the body in the waking state, your bodies while dreaming, and bodies of successive lifetimes, "all created by the self-grasping mind."

From another point of view, these bodies arise from karma, which is mental. Karma comes to fruition, ripens, and *voilà*, a body is formed. So the formation of the body comes about due to karma, which is again produced by the mind. The essence of karma, of course, is intention, which is a mental process. Again we return to the same conclusion: all of this is the product of self-grasping.

Among body, speech, and mind, the mind is all-creating. The implication here is not only that the mind has preeminence over the body, including the brain, but that it plays a fundamental role in the emergence of the universe as we know it. Whenever we observe anything in nature, either with our five physical senses or with the use of a scientific instrument of measurement or observation, all that we actually observe is appearances. On the basis of these appearances, the mind conceives of objective entities such as space, time, matter, and energy. We have no access to any of these entities as they exist in and of themselves, independently of any measurements, nor do we have any knowledge of the mind independently of conscious mental appearances. The very bifurcation of subject and object, mind and matter, is created by the conceptual mind, and none of these categories have any existence apart from the conceptual designations of minds.

The metaphysical view of scientific materialism is based on the assumption that prior to the emergence of consciousness in the universe, there was only space, time, matter, energy, and their emergent properties. So mind is naturally assumed to be solely an emergent property of biological organisms. But this assumption is challenged by no less a physicist than Stephen Hawking. Contrary to the assumptions of nineteenth-century classical physics, he has proposed that there is no absolutely objective history of the universe as it exists independently of all systems of measurement and conceptual modes of inquiry. Everything we know about the past is based on measurements we make in the present. According to quantum cosmology, every possible version of the past exists simultaneously in a state of quantum superposition. When we choose to make a measurement, we select from this range of possibilities according to the questions we are posing about the universe. When we then make the measurement, a specific array of appearances arises to our awareness, and on this basis we construct our vision of the past.[17] If scientists make only physical measurements, naturally they get only physical information, and it is on this basis that they have assumed that physical entities are more fundamental than mind or awareness. But since they have no objective means of detecting awareness in anything, awareness gets left out of their picture of the origins and evolution of the universe. This is not a limitation of nature but rather a limitation of scientific methods of inquiry that limit our vision only to objective, physical, quantifiable appearances. But to assume that the scope of the universe itself is constrained by the limitations of the methods of inquiry of modern science is a kind of religious fundamentalism.

Therefore, regarding the triad of the body, speech, and mind as well as the universe at large, this mind is the all-creating monarch. Everything we know of all of reality consists of appearances to the mind, which is formless and which takes on the appearance of everything. Among body, speech, and mind, this mind is the most important.

"A mindless body is nothing more than a corpse, so it has no power. When the body and mind separate, experiences of joy and sorrow—reaching up to the state of enlightenment or down to the three realms of samsara—are all due to mental consciousness delusively engaging with objects. Therefore the mind is certainly the agent.

Now Great Boundless Emptiness begins to elaborate, tying in body and speech. At death, when the body and mind separate, "experiences of joy and sorrow—reaching up to the state of enlightenment or down to the three realms of samsara" (the desire, form, and formless realms)—"are all due to mental consciousness delusively engaging with objects." There is no delusion in the state of enlightenment. He is saying that joys and sorrows are all due to mental consciousness delusively engaging with objects. So "the mind is certainly the agent."

"Likewise for speech: Whatever appears to be voiced is nothing more than appearances to the mind. Speech has no existence other than the conceptualizing mind's creation of the appearance of vocal expression, so the mind is most important. When the body, speech, and mind are separated, one by one, the mind continues, the body becomes a corpse, and the speech vanishes altogether. Therefore the mind is definitely the most important.

Without perception, there are no appearances of light and color, only invisible electromagnetic fields traveling through space. Even the information we have of such fields is an appearance to the mind. Without speech you can still have a mind, but without the mind there is no speech. Since the mind continues when body, speech, and mind are separated, he makes a very strong case here as to why the mind is so important and why it might be good to have the mind as your path, rather than relying primarily on physical and verbal kinds of spiritual practice.

"Here is the way the body, speech, and mind are established as indistinguishable: In the practice of the stage of generation, your own body, speech, and mind are regarded as displays of the vajra body, speech, and mind of your personal deity. In this way, you purify them and attain liberation. If they were separate, both the immutable vajra of the body and the unimpeded vajra of speech would be left behind when the mind is drawn away. Then, when the assembly of the three vajras disintegrates, wouldn't the deity perish? Therefore, rather than being separate, the many are determined to be of one taste. It follows that these three are none other than the mind: they are ascertained to be the mind alone, and this is the best and highest understanding."

Although he began by viewing them as distinct, Great Boundless Emptiness now presents a way of seeing body, speech, and mind as indistinguishable. This touches on the stage of generation, with its deeper understanding of body, speech, and mind. "*Vajra* body, speech, and mind" just means the enlightened body, speech, and mind of the deity. Through the practice of the stage of generation, "you purify them and attain liberation." If your body, speech, and mind in their deeper nature were separate, the deity would perish, but that doesn't occur. In the generation-stage practice of Vajrayana, you can be fully present, with a visualization of the vajra body, reciting the mantra with vajra speech, and maintaining divine pride, vajra mind. However, you can stop reciting the mantra at any time. You can also withdraw the visualization at any time. So the mind can be drawn away from the speech, and the mind can be drawn away from the body. Your vajra body, vajra speech, and vajra mind are of one taste, just like the nirmanakaya, sambhogakaya, and dharmakaya—distinct, but of one taste. So these three, at this deeper level of pure vision, are indistinguishable.

On the mundane level, the body, speech, and mind are distinguishable. The coarse, or ordinary mind, of an individual arises partially in dependence upon the body, and so does the speech. At a superficial level, the body seems to be primary, for neither the coarse mind of a human being nor speech can arise independently of the body. However, at death, the coarse mind doesn't simply vanish into nothing but rather dissolve backs into its source, the substrate consciousness. That subtle dimension of mind is primary. This question is being answered not only from a mundane perspective, that of an ordinary individual, but also from the perspective of pure vision. From the perspectives of both ordinary perception, for which the body and mind are separate, and of pure vision, where the body, speech, and mind are indivisible, the mind is still primary. So these three are none other than the mind. They are of one taste. How is this so?

They are united in the same way that the nirmanakaya is a manifestation of the sambhogakaya, which in turn is a manifestation of dharmakaya. That means that among the three *kayas*, dharmakaya is primary, because the other ones emerge from this absolute ground awareness and have no existence apart from the mind of the Buddha. From the perspective of pure vision, the stage of generation, vajra body and speech are none other than the mind. "They are ascertained to be the mind alone," just as sambhogakaya and nirmanakaya are ascertained to be nothing other than appearances of, the effulgence of, dharmakaya. As the bodhisattva comments, "this is the best and highest understanding."

THE EMPTINESS OF MIND

> Again the Teacher asked, "Do you, as the all-creating monarch, have form or not? If you do, what type of being's form does yours resemble? Do you, the monarch, have eyes, ears, a nose, a tongue, and a mental faculty or not? If so, where do they presently exist? What are they? Moreover, is your form round, rectangular, semicircular, triangular, many-sided, or some other kind of shape? Are you white, yellow, red, green, variegated in color, or not? If you are, by all means let me see this directly with my eyes or touch it with my hands!

As the text continues, the tables are turned once again, with the Teacher posing questions to the bodhisattva. In fact in the Tibetan tradition, and especially in the meditative context, the students rarely have an opportunity to ask questions. Rather, the teacher is always questioning the students.

The Teacher asks if the all-creating monarch—the mind—has form. Bear in mind the context, the agent, the one who's really doing the observing. Does *that* have form or not? If so, what sort of form? Here we might be tempted to say, "I know the right answer! No form, no shape, no color." But this is not a rhetorical question. Notice how the Teacher takes it from here:

> **"If you conclude that none of these exist, you may have fallen into the extreme of nihilism. So consider samsara and nirvana, joy and sorrow, appearances and the mind, and all their substantial causes, and show me their real nature."**

Concluding that you, the observer, don't have faculties, don't have shape, form, and so forth, may be an expression of the extreme of nihilism, a wrong view that undermines confidence in cause and effect.

The reference here to "substantial causes" is not reification. There is the danger that you could very easily see such a cause as some "real substance" that transforms into something, but that is not the meaning of *substantial cause*. Buddhist philosophy speaks of two kinds of causes, substantial, or primary, causes and cooperative conditions. A substantial cause, simply put, transforms into its substantial effect; it does not imply the inherent existence of cause and effect or that one inherently existent entity is transforming into another.

Take the following example: An orchid flower is a product. Something transformed into it, as any physicist will tell you. It didn't arise from nothing. There are various molecules and nutrients and so forth that transformed into this orchid, and eventually this orchid is going to flower. Later this flower is going to dry up, and at some point it is going to cease being a flower. It will turn to dust, and the dust will disperse, and so on. The Buddhist notion of substantial causes and effects parallels the physicist's theory of the conservation of mass-energy: things always emerge from something prior and turn into something else later. Nothing ever arises from nothing or transforms into nothing.

At what point does this appearance become a "flower," and when does it cease being one? A little while back this flower was something we would call a "bud." If we pried it open, we wouldn't see a flower, just some stuff that will eventually be transformed into a flower. Once this flower has dried up, has it then ceased to be a flower? If it still has some of the essential parts that contribute to what we call a flower—the petals, stamen, pistil, and so forth—we might call it a "dried flower." So it would still be a flower. Later, when the parts have separated into smaller fragments, and certainly when it has turned into dust that the wind may blow around, we would no longer call it a "flower." So this set of appearances ceases to be a flower when we withdraw its designation as such—just as the bud transformed into a flower when we withdrew the first designation and made the second.

Furthermore, there are many things that contribute to the formation of something but don't actually transform into it. If this flower was cultivated in a greenhouse, the greenhouse was a cooperative condition—as were the temperature of the room, the humidity of the room, the person who built the greenhouse, that person's parents, and the idea, "I think I'd like to go into the flower business. I'll invest my money in a greenhouse." That thought, "I'm going to go into the flower business," is a cooperative condition leading to the eventual growth of the flower, as were the sequences of situations and thoughts that gave rise to that thought and the person's grandparents and great grandparents, and back and back and so on. An infinite array or collection of cooperative conditions has come together to enable this flower to be here right now. Many of these cooperative conditions didn't transform into it, as the water and energy from the sunlight and mulch did, but nevertheless, had they not arisen, this flower wouldn't be here.

If it is a lovely flower and still quite fresh, not even brown on the edges yet, I presume it might elicit some sense of beauty from a viewer. The molecules of the flower didn't transform into your enjoyment or satisfaction. Nevertheless they contributed to it. So, just as there were many substantial causes that flowed into the flower and cooperative conditions enabling that transition to take place, the flower in turn is continually transforming into successive flowers as it exists from moment to moment.

Every moment each particle of the flower is in a state of flux; it is transforming into the particles of the flower of the next moment. So right now it is churning, churning, every particle arising and passing, giving rise to the subsequent particles—mass-energy configurations here on the one hand and, on the other hand, emanating rays of light that provoke chemical reactions in your brain. If you were viewing this flower, all of that is contributing to your perception, such as your perception of the colors of the orchid. The flower is not transforming into your perception any more than your brain is transforming into your perception. Otherwise your brain would lose weight over time, as it "transforms" into immaterial perceptions of color and pleasure and enjoyment. No, the photons being emitted from the flower are acting as cooperative conditions for your mental perception, your emotional response. Then your emotional response might give rise to a thought such as, "Ah, I think I'd like to go into the flower business." Then another cycle begins. Therefore, to assert cooperative conditions and substantial causes doesn't mean that you have to reify phenomena. The appearance of phenomena does not imply the absolute reality of the objects we conceptually impute on those appearances.

Returning to the text: "So consider samsara and nirvana, joy and sorrow"—we take our joys and sorrows so seriously, they mean so much to us—"appearances and the mind"—the mind here being defined as that which experiences appearances—"and all their substantial causes." Within that broad domain can you think of anything that arises in dependence upon causes and conditions that requires only cooperative conditions and no substantial cause—nothing to transform into it? The Buddhist hypothesis is that all phenomena that arise in dependence upon causes and conditions do require something to transform into them—you never get something from nothing. There is always a substantial cause.

Consider my perception of a piece of colored cloth. Photons of light emanating from the cloth strike my retina and catalyze electrochemical events in my head. They do not transform into my immaterial perception of the cloth, but they do serve as cooperative conditions for the emergence of that perception. Only a prior continuum of awareness, which is a substantial cause, transforms into that perception. So all things that arise in dependence upon causes and conditions have both substantial causes and cooperative conditions. Material things never serve as substantial causes of immaterial events, such as thoughts and perceptions; and immaterial things do not act as substantial causes of material things.

Now, consider samsara and nirvana, joy and sorrow. Where does your joy really come from? Not from cooperative conditions. Not from candy, nor guacamole, nor from sourdough bread—not from any of these things that may or may not catalyze them. All your joys and sorrows arise from your mind, with prior moments of awareness acting as substantial causes for subsequent states of consciousness.

When the Teacher asks the bodhisattva to show him the "real nature" of samsara and nirvana, joy and sorrow, appearances and awareness, and all their substantial causes, he is referring to their phenomenological nature. This is what scientists, psychologists, and meditators study—myriad phenomena arising in dependence upon causes and conditions, each arising from its substantial cause. The Teacher is focusing once more on the theme of the mind, the agent, which we can simply call the self, the observer, the one who acts, what is generally known as "I."

> Great Boundless Emptiness responded, "O Teacher, Bhagavan, the self has no form, so it is empty of form. Likewise, it has no sound, smell, taste, touch, or mental attribute, so it is empty of each of these. It is devoid of shape and color, so it is empty of them. It is certain that the eyes, ears, nose, tongue, and mental faculty have no existence apart from limpid, clear consciousness itself. Without nihilistically reducing them to nonexistence, the indeterminate manifestations of samsara and nirvana appear like a magician's illusions. Therefore, I have come to the conclusion that the agent has only the quality of being unceasing."

"Empty" means "devoid of." The self, the observer, the agent is empty of form. "Likewise, it has no sound, smell, taste, touch, or mental attribute" of its own, in its own nature, "so it is empty of each of these." The sensory faculties of sight, sound, smell, taste, and mental awareness also have no existence apart from consciousness. Interactions among external physical stimuli and the brain are not enough to produce these experiences. "Indeterminate manifestations" means all manner of manifestations, many of them unpredictable. You just never know what's coming up. For example, sometimes, for no apparent or identifiable reason, you simply experience a sense of well-being. Many things happen inexplicably, "like a magician's illusions." Who is the magician? The mind. What's the magic? All that rises to the mind.

Great Boundless Emptiness comes to the conclusion that the agent "has only the quality of being unceasing." That's merely his answer for the time being. Now, is this conclusion a blind alley, a red herring, or is this the way things *really* are? Thus we come to one of the core themes, one of the principal heuristic devices of the Buddhist tradition as a whole, which boils down to this: There is no external, absolute authority for the sutras and tantras indicating which statements are definitive and which are provisional. We are not told, "Just memorize this, and by doing so you will know all the teachings to be taken literally—this is the way things really are. Those other teachings were only expedient means for guiding specific disciples at a particular point in their spiritual evolution." There is no such teacher's aid—and there mustn't be one. If we relied upon something of that sort, we wouldn't achieve enlightenment. We would only become obedient memorizers.

This difficulty appears especially when we grapple with common cosmological descriptions in Buddhism, such as "Mount Meru and its surrounding continents and subcontinents." Are things really like that? Is that a correct geography or simply a lovely metaphorical image? We must continue to grapple with that. Düdjom Lingpa said he had lived on one of these subcontinents. Perhaps it's not just a metaphor, not merely poetry. As another example, in the *Heart Sutra* it says, with respect to emptiness, that there is no form, no sound, and so on. With respect to emptiness there is no truth of suffering, no truth of the source of suffering, no cessation, no path. It appears that the absolute nature of the four noble truths, one of the foundations of the Buddha's teachings, is being questioned there. These exemplify a continual challenge to our intelligence, a built-in mechanism in Buddhism to prevent us from becoming fundamentalists, from mistaking the raft for the far shore, from confusing the finger that points to the moon with the moon itself. If it weren't for this approach, we might easily say, "I know Buddhism very well," and then recite it all by rote and say, with missionary zeal, "Because I have memorized all the words and believe them, I am saved!"

The Buddhist tradition bends over backward to prevent this from happening. Some teachings are provisional, some are definitive, and it is up to us in each day and in each step of our spiritual maturation to reassess which is which. So is the statement "the agent has only the quality of being unceasing" definitive or provisional? It is essential that each of us take this back to our cushion and meditate on these words. When you attend to the agent, the observer, do you detect an unceasing quality? Do you agree or disagree with Great Boundless Emptiness?

> The Bhagavan asked, "O Vajra of Mind, tell me, when you first arose, what was your source? Did you come from the earth and water, from fire, and from air and space, or did you originate from the four cardinal directions, the eight directions, or from above or below? Investigate whence you arose and that which arises, and analyze! Likewise, investigate where you are now and what you are, and analyze!

"Vajra of Mind" here means "unceasing mind." *Vajra* is the immutable, the enduring, the impenetrable, the adamantine. In a sense, the Teacher is applying a characterization or nickname to Great Boundless Emptiness.

"Likewise, investigate where you are now and what you are" and analyze them! This may not be comfortable. There are some sharp edges here. As you analyze you may encounter the afflictive emotions, the turbulence and cacophony of the mind. You may seek relief in shamatha, in the peace of that mentally dormant state. But shamatha only pacifies, it doesn't liberate.

> "If this so-called mind were located in the head, when a thorn pierced the foot, for instance, there would be no reason to experience a sharp pain. If it were located in the feet, why would there be discomfort even if the head and limbs were amputated? Suppose it were located in the body as a whole. In that case, if unbearable regret or misery were to arise in the mind when an external item— an article of clothing, a cup, a house, or some other possession—is taken away or destroyed by others, the mind would have to be located in them. If it were located inside the body, there would be

no one who identified with things outside. If it were located outside, there would be no one inside to cling or grasp on to the body. If it is presently located in the body, where will it be located when it separates from the body? On what will it depend?

Now the Teacher presents hypotheses, possibilities to investigate. The so-called mind is the observer—that which attends to, understands, knows appearances. You may identify with this so-called mind as "you"; for aren't you the one who knows, who observes appearances?

Suppose you have a prized vase and then somebody comes along and shatters it. In response you shudder and weep, and maybe you go on grieving for a long time. Was your mind located in the vase that was shattered? If not, why did you shudder? Why do you grieve? Why do you hurt? Is your mind located there? Maybe that precious heirloom is a piece of clothing, or a porcelain cup, or your great grandparents' house, or an antique car. Suppose you can't pay the mortgage on the house and it's taken away, or it's simply destroyed; you see your house go up in flames. As that happens, do you feel yourself burning? Is the mind located in the house? Is that why you're suffering so much regret and misery? "If it," this mind, "were located inside the body, there would be no one who identified with things outside." If you are really in here—in your body—then your house can burn up, the heirlooms can be shattered, and it shouldn't be a problem. As far as you're concerned, that stuff is out there and you're in here.

So where exactly are you located? "If it," the mind, "were located outside, there would be no one inside to cling or grasp on to the body." Yet of course we do. If you step on my hand, I say "ouch," thinking, "That's my body." If you do think your mind is inside your body, ask "in which part is it located?" Can it be located throughout, permeating your whole body? In that case, when the mind separates from the body, where is it located then? On what will it depend? That question applies both to death and to sleep. In dreams you experience yourself being in another environment, and often you seem to have a body. Where is the mind vis-à-vis the body lying in bed? Is it inside that body or outside? Is it nowhere at all? If so, what can that mean?

To recap, the fundamental questions here are: Did you arise? Whence did you arise? If you think you weren't always here, if you think you are arising in some way—whether as a "hum," or maybe afresh, perhaps differently from moment to moment—then where did you come from? Where are you now? What are you now? Little questions like that!

Up to this point Bodhisattva Great Boundless Emptiness has answered Samantabhadra's question about the true nature of samsara and nirvana, joy and sorrow, appearances and the mind, and so on with, "I have come to the conclusion that the agent has only the quality of being unceasing." Then the Teacher has challenged him to probe more deeply because his initial answer is just one more conceptual superimposition. We are trying to move beyond that, beyond all of our habitual notions and learned ideas and so forth so that we can go right to direct perception and report from there.

"If it," the mind, "is presently located in the body," which many people believe, "where will it be located when it separates from the body? On what will it depend?" These are marvelous questions. Many people, including scientists who study the mind-brain nexus, have an immediate answer for that. They would say the mind is presently located in the body, specifically in the brain. Where will it be located when it separates from the body? It doesn't separate from the body. When the brain dies the mind vanishes. Of course they have no hard, scientific proof that this is so. Is there empirical evidence to the contrary, suggesting that the mind can separate from the body?

In the West there are several areas that suggest strongly that the mind can do just that. There are reports of out-of-body experiences, studied by Bruce Greyson for example, and detailed accounts of children allegedly recalling their past-life experiences, as studied meticulously by Ian Stevenson.[18] We also have the reports from yogis. In the Tibetan Buddhist tradition there are teachings that enable you to create a special dream body. It can be generated by means of completion-stage practice, and with it you can launch out into the universe and travel around. According to accounts by Tibetan yogis, you can experience valid perceptions of things that are far away while your normal body is fast asleep. So this is not just a lucid dream but a special dream body that goes wherever you direct the mind. You can visit pure lands, your home state, any place, and see it as if your eyes were actually there, hear it as if your ears were there.[19]

When the mind separates from the body, it might travel in a special dream body or, once the body dies, enter the after-death bardo. "On what does it depend?" We have described here a three-tiered model of the mind: the psyche, the substrate consciousness, and, at the deepest level, primordial consciousness, or rigpa. There are numerous examples of both yogis and ordinary people who have been able to access rigpa in such a way as to achieve supernormal powers such as clairvoyance and clairaudience. Since rigpa is beyond both space and time, this is a possible basis for such experiences.

> "Directly point out the body, face, and location of the one who is present. Investigate the location and environment, along with the size and so forth, of this being that is in charge. Look! Finally, you must investigate the act of going and the one who goes; so observe the destination, path, and point of departure of the mind—the one doing everything—and watch how it moves. If you see the act of going and the one who goes, show me the size, form, shape, and color of the one who goes."

Continuing along the same lines, once more the Buddha, the Bhagavan, challenges Great Boundless Emptiness to point out the agent and its surroundings. He doesn't mean "think about it"—he wants observation, empirical investigation. "Finally, you must investigate the act of going and the one who goes." Go someplace, but have nothing on your mind apart from the sheer event of going, and let that be the sole focus of your attention. What does it mean to go, to walk, for example? As you are walking, choose a destination, observe the destination, and then observe the path to get there and the "point of departure of the mind." Notice "the one doing everything— and watch how it moves."

This is not like close application of mindfulness of the body within the practice of the four applications of mindfulness. There you are observing your body—your feet in touch with the ground, body movements, sensations, and so forth. This is much more subtle. The referent of the word "it" is the mind. Watch how the mind moves. We're really interested in the nature of this agent, and this is the fundamental theme of Dzogchen. Let's just stick with the mind. Let's understand the mind, fathom the mind, plumb the depths of the mind. Everything else will be revealed as a consequence. The Buddha said, "All phenomena are preceded by the mind. When the mind is comprehended, all phenomena are comprehended."[20]

"If you see the act of going and the one who goes, show me the size, form, shape, and color of the one who goes." Consider that when you're not being cautious, not being grilled on this question, you have the sensation that wherever you are going, that is where your mind is going, too, right? If you are here, your mind is also. It isn't over yonder. So if you have the sense that your mind is in motion, observe exactly *how* the mind is in motion. What is the nature of the mind that's in motion as it goes from here to there? Look!

> Great Emptiness responded, "O Teacher, Bhagavan, I have no eyes,
> so there is nothing that appears to me as form. Likewise, I have no
> ears, so there is nothing that appears to me as sound. I have no nose,
> so there is nothing that appears to me as smell. I have no tongue, so
> there is nothing that appears to me as taste. I have no body, so there
> is nothing that appears to me as touch, either.

The bodhisattva, who is a very quick study, rises to the challenge by looking not into a mirror but directly into the nature of awareness itself. He has withdrawn his awareness, because if you have your eyes wide open, of course there is form. The Buddha has directed him, however, to ignore external phenomena, the body and so forth, and to probe the nature of the mind. Let's imagine Great Boundless Emptiness has the power of samadhi, or focused concentration, and can draw the full force of awareness away from the physical senses, away from visual forms, sound, and so forth—draw it purely into the domain of the mind, perhaps even right into the domain of the substrate consciousness. From that perspective he says, "I have no eyes, so there is nothing that appears to me as form." In his present mode of awareness, there are no forms, likewise for the appearances of the other senses. This is an experience similar to deep sleep, but *luminous* deep sleep.

"Therefore, because I lack the five senses and their appearances, there is no I that arises. If the one who arises is not established as being real, then from this time onward, the so-called mind is not established as real either and is therefore nonexistent. Until now, there should have been something bearing attributes, called this being. Since I am unoriginated emptiness, the source of my origination is empty. As to seeking the source, earth is something I have created. Similarly, all phenomena, including water, fire, air, and space, are nothing other than apparitions of self-grasping alone. This implies that the I that arises is nowhere to be found.

One interpretation that may apply here is that Great Boundless Emptiness has withdrawn entirely into the substrate consciousness. There the five senses are completely dormant, as are the other mental faculties. There the sense of I itself is dormant. "If the one who arises"—the I, self, or agent—"is not established as being real, then from this time onward, the so-called mind is not established as real either and is therefore nonexistent." When you are abiding in the substrate consciousness, you've temporarily lost your mind. Your psyche is not there. Your self is not there explicitly. It has become dormant because there are no appearances. Even the mind itself was only an apparition, and therefore it is nonexistent—nonexistent as in "not truly existent." It doesn't have any true, inherent existence of its own. It is only an appearance.

Through observation the bodhisattva couldn't find any entity-bearing attributes—"this being." Saying "Since I am unoriginated emptiness," he now begins to define himself; but continue to consider the possibilities for interpretation here: "the source of my origination is empty." In other words, "I'm not originating. I'm not coming from anywhere." Asked if he arose from earth, "on the contrary," he responds. Earth is something he has created, conceptually imputed upon appearances of solidity and firmness. "Similarly, all phenomena, including water, fire, air, and space, are nothing other than apparitions of self-grasping alone."

Bear in mind that the word "self" here could refer not only to the self of a person but to the identity of any phenomenon. Something arises, and then we impute earth, water, fire, air, space, and so forth to that arising phenomenon, and by that imputation it comes into existence. "This implies that the I that arises is nowhere to be found." A sense of self does arise, but out of what? How deep is his realization here? He doesn't tell us; he is just giving us his experience.

Consider two possibilities, the first being: Through the practice of shamatha, he has arrived at the substrate consciousness. There is no "I"; there are no physical sensations. The mental experiences of a sense of personal identity and so forth are all simply arising as manifestations or apparitions of the substrate consciousness. It's empty—"I am unoriginated emptiness." He is not finding any origin or basis from which the substrate consciousness emerges. Furthermore, all subsequent appearances in the waking state, when he's engaging with physical reality, are merely apparitions of the substrate, the empty, luminous space of the mind. Just as all sensory and mental appearances arise from this space, so do all subjective mental processes of the coarse mind arise from the substrate consciousness. What is the nature of the appearances arising? As they appear we lock on to them, we cast them within our conceptual grid filled with definitions and language, and we say, "Ah, that's earth, that's water, fire, air, space," and everything else. The term for this is *self-grasping*, whether it's directed toward yourself, other people, or other phenomena. As you approach the apparent location of the reified object and finally arrive at that place, there's nothing. There never was anything, only an appearance of it being there.

Here is the other possibility regarding the depth of the bodhisattva's experience: When he says, "I am unoriginated emptiness," he may have actually experienced *shunyata*, emptiness, which is much deeper than the substrate. Has he broken all the way through and fathomed the ultimate nature of reality, seen directly that all phenomena are dependently related events, each one devoid of, empty of, any inherent nature of its own? Can we tell?

Now he identifies himself. Where does he abide?

"I am the nonabiding nature of emptiness, so there is no place I dwell.
As for the so-called body: Sores, swelling, goiters, ulcers, and so on

may arise in the body that appears in the waking state, but they are not present in the dream body. And sores, swelling, goiters, and ulcers that appear to afflict the body and limbs in a dream are absent in the waking state. During the waking state, the body may be wounded or beaten as punishment by a king, but this does not appear on the dream body. If it happens in a dream, it is not present on the body in the waking state. Similarly, location, environment, and their possessor, whether they appear to be outside or are grasped as being inside, are all nothing more than my own appearances.

"Therefore I do not abide in either external or internal phenomena, nor do external or internal phenomena abide in me. They are apparitions of self-grasping, like a magician's illusion, but they are not created intentionally, as in the case of a magician and his magic. The self arises, so external appearances arise automatically, but they have no location. Even if you investigate the agent and the destination, the one who moves and the destination have no objective existence, so they do not go with the nature of me and mine.

For the time being let's maintain the hypothesis that he is referring to the substrate consciousness and nothing more. Is there anything here indicating that he's referring to something beyond that? From the perspective of the substrate consciousness, the appearance of your body in the waking state is neither more nor less real than your body in the dream state or in the after-death bardo because these appearances all emerge from the substrate. The so-called physical body can have sores and illness and so on in the waking state, but they are not present in the dream body. You can have a perfectly good body in the dream state no matter how malformed your body is in the waking state and have yet another body with different characteristics in the after-death bardo. Those are three different bodies, all arising from the same source, but what happens in one is not necessarily happening in the others. In fact, they are usually different.

"All phenomena appear, yet they are not other than the domain of the self. Moreover, as the body, speech, and mind have never existed separately, their appearances are of the same taste. In all waking appearances, dream appearances, and appearances after this life, the body, speech, and mind are indistinguishable from me. So this is certain: the one who goes and the destination are not real phenomena."

When Great Boundless Emptiness says that all phenomena are not other than the domain of the self, is he referring to rigpa? Has he gone that deep? I still see no evidence yet that he's gone beyond the substrate consciousness. He has already spoken of how the mind can leave the body and speech can become mute, so in a way they are distinct. However, what he must mean here is that all experiences of speech are never separate from the mind. They are no more than expressions, appearances to the mind. Likewise, all experiences of the body are no more than appearances of mind. We have never had any contact with our own or anyone else's body or speech that existed separately or apart from our own minds. All you ever experience are appearances to the mind.

How can we experience the appearances of body, speech, and mind as one taste? One way is, when doing the simple practice of mindfulness of breathing, to on occasion let your awareness suffuse the whole body, but with as little conceptual superimposition as possible. Let go of imagining what you think your body looks like. See if you can set aside all the superimpositions based upon memory of your body's appearance and let your awareness be as naked as possible. Simply observe what's being presented to the tactile sense, moment to moment—the rhythms, the buzzing, the tingling, the movements. While you are attending in that way, observing the rhythm of the in- and out-breaths, you may also become aware of thoughts and images. It may then occur to you that these thoughts and images are not happening at a location different from your body. The body to which you are attending is not demarcated with one area having tactile sensations and images, while thoughts occur someplace else. The domain of experience of the body is simply a subset of the domain of experience of the mind. They are neither separate nor adjacent. All experience of the body is nothing more than sensations arising to the mind.

In similar fashion the bodhisattva says that the appearances of body, speech, and mind in the waking state, in dreams, and after death "are indistinguishable from me." That is, they do not exist apart from me, separate from me, of another nature from me. What is the referent of *me* here? I maintain that he is referring only to the substrate consciousness.

MIND'S ESSENTIAL NATURE

The Bhagavan commented, "O Vajra of Mind, investigate the dimensions of your so-called mind; then determine and recognize its essential nature. Are external space and the internal mind the same or different? If they are the same, the essential nature of the mind must be space. If they are different, you would have to agree that space in a dream, space in the daytime, and space after this life are not the same but different. If the earlier space ceases and later types of space arise, one after the other, each space would be subject to transformation, creation, and destruction. In that case, determine the causes and conditions from which they arise. If space actually appears in the daytime due to the sun rising in the morning, doesn't the sun cause it to appear in a dream and after this life? Or is it the clear light of your own mind? Don't just give this lip service; instead, penetrate it with certainty."

Recall that the Teacher—the Lake-Born Vajra, Padmasambhava, Samantabhadra—is addressing the bodhisattva who said that when he looks within, what he sees has "the quality of being unceasing." Also bear in mind the overall context to this point: Show us the path to liberation...the path with which we may "achieve the state of the fully perfected Buddha Samantabhadra in one lifetime and with one body." And the teaching being given takes the mind as the path as preliminary for ascertaining the ultimate nature of phenomena, emptiness, which is then taken as the path leading to the realization of buddha nature.

If you are going to take the mind as your path, you must get a good sense of what it is. What is this so-called mind? Does it have shape, color, or

size? Find the dimensions of your so-called mind, "then determine and recognize its essential nature." What is it about your mind that makes it your
mind rather than something else? If I say, "Make your Hawaiian shirt your
path," you must know how to recognize that Hawaiian shirt amid everything else. It's as prosaic as that. There are certain defining characteristics
of a Hawaiian shirt by which you can identify it from other things. If you
know the defining characteristics you go right through your wardrobe and
pick it out.

In teachings on the mind, the word "space" comes up rather frequently.
Upon examination you may see boundless space, empty space, luminous
space, or black space—deep space. "Are external space and the internal
mind the same or different?" This is the Buddha once again interrogating
Great Boundless Emptiness. Let's identify external space experientially. You
can see it, can't you? Look over yonder. Can you see the space between
yourself and another person? If you look out a window at mountains in the
distance, can you see the space between yourself and the mountains over
there? Not only can you see the mountains way over yonder, but you can
see the space. Everyone can. That's what we call space—that emptiness
between you and me or you and the mountains. Moreover that space is
limpid and clear.

We are more likely to attend to the objects we view than the space
around them because we have those habits and imprints. Some of them are
from our previous lives but others are from our body—the genes we have
inherited from our forbears, our parents—along with the behavioral examples they've given us. So we have two tracks operating here—that of evolution and that of the individual substrate consciousness—merging together
into what we call a "human life."

From the evolutionary track we are well prepared to be able to ascertain,
identify, and engage specifically with things that are moving. This has
helped us survive. If something intends to eat you, and if you intend to
avoid being eaten, or if you yourself are after prey, movement is of the
utmost importance. We are geared to identify movement quickly. If you
were gazing out at some vast valley and there was somebody down there
holding very still five hundred yards away, you probably wouldn't see him.

If that person moves a tiny bit, however, you will notice. You pick him out, identify him, and see that he is there. So we are geared for movement, and more broadly speaking we are geared to identify objects, because if there's something out there to eat, to run away from, or to mate with, it is going to be an object—something in space. Our senses, then, are geared to identify, focus on, and thereby reify objects, especially those that move. From an evolutionary or biological perspective, that helps us to survive and procreate.

We also operate from a variety of perspectives or influences—spiritual and psychological, as well as biological. In the words of William James: "For the moment, what we attend to is reality."[21] For the reasons I've mentioned, most of the time we are attending to objects; they are our reality. So if space is to become real for you, you have to attend to it. It is not something that we are naturally wired to do from a biological perspective. Nevertheless, we can do it. We can develop that habit, become more and more familiar with attending to space. In so doing, space will become more real for us.

Now we have this fascinating question: "Are external space and the internal mind the same or different?" When speaking of the internal mind, the Bhagavan is not saying the mind is really inside. He is referring to the way we think of an "outside world" versus the world we experience when we close our eyes and look "inside." We have the sense that the mind is somehow within, rather than existing in external space. Now, are they the same or different?

"If they are the same, the essential nature of the mind must be space." That's one possibility. On the other hand, "if they are different, you would have to agree that space in a dream, space in the daytime, and space after this life," for example, in the after-death bardo, "are not the same but different. If the earlier space ceases," as you go from one of these transitional phases to another—from the transitional phase of daytime experience, to that of dreamtime experience, to the phase of the bardo—then in each case a different space arises.

As you fall asleep your physical senses retract, and passing through deep sleep you emerge into another space, say dreaming. If the previous space, before falling asleep, ceases, does it simply vanish? Is it extinguished? If at one moment you are observing the space around you and then later your senses withdraw into sleep, does the previous space become nonexistent and another entirely new space arise, namely the space of dreams? If so, "each space would be subject to transformation, creation, and destruction." They would arise freshly, linger for a while, and then be destroyed. If that were the case, the Teacher challenges us to find the causes and conditions from which they arise.

In Buddhism, when you see "causes and conditions," "causes" refers to substantial causes, and "conditions" refers to cooperative conditions. Furthermore, any fruit, any consequence, arises in dependence upon at least one substantial cause and at least one cooperative condition. Consider the hypothesis that the space of a dream arises at the outset of the dream and is then destroyed when the dream comes to an end. While it is present, or as it arises, that space is a conditioned phenomenon, rising in dependence upon causes and conditions. What is the substantial cause for the space of the dream? What actually transforms into the space of the dream? By what is the space of the dream conditioned? Likewise for the space of the daytime and the space of the after-death bardo: What is transformed into them and by what are they conditioned? Determine the causes and conditions from which those three types of space arise. Consider that just as various mental states and processes arise from the substrate consciousness throughout the waking state, the dream state, and in the bardo, so do all experiences of space arise from the continuum substrate, which flows throughout all these experiences. None of these appearances of space or its contents is any more real than the others. These simply arise from and disappear back into this flow of the space of the mind.

Moving on to the next question, if the sun, as an external source of illumination out there in space, is necessary as a cooperative condition to illuminate ordinary space, so that it actually manifests, then shouldn't there also be an external source in a dream that illuminates its space as a cooperative condition and a similar source in the after-death bardo?

What does physics tell us about the light supposedly emanating from the sun? We can view light as either electromagnetic waves or as photon particles. Looking at light as particles—that is, as photons—the nuclear activity of the sun emits an enormous quantity of them at various frequencies and in all directions. Physics says that these wave or particle "light" emissions from the sun are not bright, they have no color. By themselves, they don't look like anything. They are not self-illuminating.

The sun in and of itself is not yellow, nor are the photons being distributed by it yellow, nor is the sun intrinsically bright, nor are the photons bright, nor are the electromagnetic waves distributed by the sun bright. So where is all of this light we see coming from? Sentient beings possess eyes and all of the visual hardware connecting the retina to the visual cortex. When those invisible photons strike the retina, they trigger a complex sequence of electrochemical events—though the process is poorly understood by science—and the end result is the perception of light.

So we could say that the photons coming into our eyes and the sequence of electrochemical events from the retina back to the visual cortex are all cooperative conditions for the experience of light. Nothing in the head is bright—not the retina, not the optic nerve, not the visual cortex. When all of these electrochemical events in the brain, stimulated by the photons of very specific frequencies (hence seeing yellow, red, and so forth), act as cooperative conditions, they then influence the flow of visual perception.

Thus visual perception arises—but from what? What is the substantial cause of visual perception? It is the preceding continuum of visual perception, or if you just woke up, it emerges from the substrate consciousness. A stream of mental awareness—the substantial cause—transforms into visual perception, which is then conditioned by the electrochemical events in the brain, which in turn are influenced by photons coming in from the outside environment.

We now arrive at a very interesting conclusion: in order to appear, light and color require consciousness. This has in fact been known by science for centuries—back to the time of Descartes and even a lot earlier. Descartes, Galileo, and many other pioneers of the scientific revolution drew a distinction between "secondary attributes," such as light and sound that arise only relative to sensory perception, and "primary attributes," such as location and mass that exist independently of sensory perception. Color and light, being secondary attributes, don't exist without consciousness. So consciousness is actually the source of illumination, making all appearances to the senses manifest. The photons and all the electrochemical events in the brain are merely cooperative conditions allowing consciousness to illuminate in specific ways—as gold, as red, as blue, and so on. When we gaze at the sun, what we are seeing, metaphorically speaking, is the light of consciousness. Were there no consciousness the sun would be invisible. It would not be light, it would not be bright, and it certainly would not be yellow. There is something about the particular types of cooperative conditions coming from the sun that enable the light of consciousness to blaze so brilliantly. The source of illumination of the sun is the observing mind, and it is the same for candles, and lamps, and any other source of illumination. They are simply expressions of the radiance of awareness.

So, returning to our question, could it be that there is a single source that illuminates space, be it in the waking state, in the dream state, or in the after-death bardo, namely, the innate luminosity of your own awareness—"the clear light of your own mind?" "Don't just give this lip service," says the Bhagavan, and don't believe what I have just suggested on my authority; "instead, penetrate it with certainty." Pursue it. Pursue it experientially, pursue it cognitively, but come to certainty: What is illuminating the world and what gives rise to space?

> Great Boundless Emptiness responded, "O Teacher, Bhagavan, the essential nature of my mind is definitely space. During the daytime, earth, water, fire, air, oneself, others, form, sound, smell, taste, touch, and mental objects are displayed in the domain of space, grasped by the conceptual mind. In dream appearances as well, the ground of the mind appears as space, and the entire world, its inhabitants, and sense objects are all displayed as they were before. After this life too, the essential nature of the mind appears as space, and in that domain the entire world, its inhabitants, and sense objects appear in the same way: they are held by the mind, and one is deluded over and over again.

Again, here the bodhisattva is speaking not of the mind's ultimate nature but its relative characteristics by means of which you can identify mind versus that which is not mind. The objects of the mind "are displayed in the domain of space, grasped by the conceptual mind." Recall that all grasping is not necessarily reification. All the gradations of grasping boil down to two main categories: grasping where standard conceptual designations are used to communicate but where no reification is implied and grasping where reification does take place. The grasping to which the bodhisattva refers is of the first category. So objects of the mind are displayed—they reveal themselves—and are grasped; that is, they are identified as such. "This is form, this is smell, taste, earth, water." The act of designating is performed by the conceptual mind.

Likewise in dreams "the entire world," the entire dream world, "its inhabi-tants, and sense objects are all displayed as they were before." That is, they seem to arise very similarly to the way they arise in the waking state. In this environment they are clearly arising in the space of the mind. "After this life, too"—here he's referring specifically to the after-death bardo—"the essential nature of the mind appears as space, and in that domain the entire world, its inhabitants, and sense objects appear in the same way." Keep in mind that the world of the after-death bardo overlaps with our world. For instance, there are ghosts floating around, looking at their dead bodies or seeing their grieving relatives. This is why, from the Tibetan tradition, for up to seven weeks after a person has died, if you think of that person, it is believed that he or she may perceive those thoughts. Ghosts are clairvoyant. So when you think of them, do so with benevolent thoughts and help them on their way.

Whenever grasping occurs, chances are, out of sheer habit, that one is continually deluded. Why? By first reifying and then following our "natural" habitual patterns, manifestations of craving and aversion and all the mental afflictions ensue, resulting in deluded behavior.

> "Therefore space, self, others, and all sense objects are of one
> taste—they are certainly not separate. Moreover, it is the luminosity
> of space itself, and nothing else, that makes appearances manifest.
> The essential nature of the mind and its ground is space itself. Vari-

ous appearances occur in the realm of mental cognition—limpid,
clear, forever-present consciousness. The display of these appearances is like the reflections in a mirror or the images of planets and
stars in a pool of limpid, clear water.

Although on one level self and others and so forth are different, they are not
fundamentally, radically separate. "Moreover, it is the luminosity of space
itself," in reference to the space of the mind, "and nothing else, that makes
appearances manifest." Again, the sun, the moon, and all other external
sources of illumination are bright because your mind is bright. There is
only one source of illumination for the entire world: consciousness, which
is nondual with space. Because consciousness makes manifest, or illuminates, all the appearances that arise in the space of the mind, space itself is
said to be luminous.

Suppose you were to observe the space above a nearby object. What's
there? Empty space, right? Then imagine a round, red apple in that space.
Where did this image come from? You didn't pull it out of a shopping bag
and place it there. It emerged from the empty space of your mind and is
simply an expression of the luminosity that was already there. The luminous, empty space above the object took on the contours of an apple. It was
the luminosity of that space that allowed for the appearance of an apple.

What is the ground of your psyche? It's the substrate consciousness, the
alayavijñana. So when he speaks of space being the ground of the essential
nature of the mind, he is not referring to the ultimate ground here. He is
venturing into the domain of consciousness accessed by shamatha, not the
ultimate ground awareness that is accessed by Dzogchen. We can be sure
he is not speaking of rigpa because he speaks of the dichotomy between
external space and the internal mind.

The bodhisattva describes the realm of mental cognition as "limpid, clear,
forever-present consciousness." The mind has its own realm, its own space,
and appearances occur in that space—during the daytime, during dreaming, and during the after-death bardo. He compares those appearances to
"the reflections in a mirror or the images of planets and stars in a pool of
limpid, clear water." Those two metaphors will recur many times in this

text. Traditionally, there are ten standard metaphors illustrating the illusory nature of phenomena, and in some instances all ten of them are mentioned. Here he is using just two of them: reflections in a mirror and images of planets and stars in a pool of water.

If you hold up a mirror and look at some scene reflected there, the scene you are viewing appears to be somewhere off in the distance. As you know, however, in a mirror there is nothing "over there" that corresponds to what you are seeing and to where you are objectively focusing your attention. We typically look at a scene in a mirror, a camera lens, or directly with our eyes and believe that the object of our attention exists from its own side, but that object is empty of inherent existence. Concerning the images of the planets and stars billions of miles away, for all practical purposes there is no difference between staring at the night sky and looking into a reflecting pool at your feet. In either case, when you view reflections of, or look directly at, planets and stars, you are effectively gazing into infinity. Mirror, camera lens, and eyes—they cannot distinguish this distance from infinity. So for all practical purposes you are now gazing at infinity, looking through planet earth to the stars, and that's exactly, objectively where the image is. And the image is completely empty of any true planets or stars.

THE SOURCE OF APPEARANCES

"Once limpid, clear consciousness has withdrawn into the central domain of pervasive, empty space, it has been directed inward. At that time, the mind and all appearances disappear as they completely dissolve into an ethically neutral, pervasive void. Through the power of self-grasping, the essential nature of this great, pervasive vacuity—the basis of phenomena—arises as the mind and its thoughts. This is certain. Since space and luminosity are nothing other than the mind, the mind itself becomes self and others by the power of the contributing circumstance of its radiant clarity.

Having withdrawn from external space, away from the senses, limpid, clear, transparent, and luminous consciousness has come into itself, come into the nature of the mind—"it has been directed inward." This is what he means by directing awareness inward—away from the sense fields, away perhaps even from the objects of the mind, and right into the central domain of pervasive, empty space. At that point the mind and all appearances—your psyche—disappears. Your mind dissolves into the substrate consciousness, and all appearances dissolve into the substrate.

The substrate consciousness isn't really empty. It's like an ocean of "potential energy," from which the "kinetic energy" of the appearances of the mind emerge. Only now you have withdrawn limpid clear consciousness not only from the sense fields, but away from internal chitchat, from images—away from all of the mind's contents—such that what you experience is empty and free of appearances. At that moment your mind, your psyche, has vanished. You have lost your mind insofar as the mind is something you designate on that vast array of mental processes that characterize the mind in action. With the mind now dormant, all that remains is the ground of the mind, the substrate consciousness, that from which the mind emerges.

"At that time, the mind and all appearances disappear as they completely dissolve into an ethically neutral, pervasive void." That is precisely the substrate. The term "ethically neutral" is the tip-off. (Note that I have translated the Tibetan word *tongpa* here as "void" rather than "empty," so that the reader won't mistake it for *emptiness*.) As awareness is withdrawn from the sense fields, they disappear, they "go flat," leaving a void that is ethically neutral. Since that is the substrate, it is confirmed that what Great Boundless Emptiness has been building up to here is not Dzogchen. Rather, this has been an introduction to the practice of shamatha.

"Through the power of self-grasping," again referring not just to grasping on to the personal self but grasping on to the identity of any object, "the essential nature of this great, pervasive vacuity—the basis of phenomena—arises as the mind and its thoughts." This is not the basis of reality as a whole, but this is the basis for the continuum of your experiences from lifetime to lifetime. What is it that arouses the substrate consciousness to take on the guise of a mind—be it a human mind, a frog's mind, or a deva's mind? (The substrate consciousness itself doesn't belong exclusively to any one class of sentient beings. It manifests for beings of all the six realms). It is through the power of self-grasping that the substrate consciousness—the basis of all your experiences—manifests apparitions like a magician. "This is certain."

"Since space and luminosity are nothing other than the mind"—what he is stating here is even more astounding than the notion that the light of the sun is as expression of consciousness. He is saying that luminosity and now even space are nothing other than the mind. Furthermore, "the mind itself becomes self and others by the power of the contributing circumstance of its radiant clarity."

As I commented earlier, grasping, in and of itself, does not automatically imply reification. It is merely an act of identification. The mind reaches out and conceptually designates: "Over there, that's Jane." No mental affliction or delusion is implied. Conventionally speaking, Jane is there. By way of self-grasping, in this case grasping on to Jane's self, I am provided with objects—objects with attributes such as the color of Jane's hair, her height, talents, personal history, and so on. How does something over there have all of these things? By the power of conceptual designation. Somebody designates Jane, and as soon as there is a designation upon a basis—in this case Jane's body—I can identify her as such. What is it that enables there to be an attribute bearer, a part bearer, a clothing bearer, a mind bearer? Conceptual designation puts it all together.

Self-grasping, or conceptual designation, on the one hand and radiant clarity on the other are two different things. They are not competing; they are working together. When looking over in the direction of Jane, had the radiant clarity of my awareness not seen colors and images arising, I wouldn't be able to bring up the designation "body," nor "Jane's body," let alone "Jane." Therefore it is not a purely conceptual process that provides us with the basic appearances themselves. Also bear in mind that the radiant clarity of awareness does not refer exclusively to the visual mode. The luminosity of awareness also manifests as smells, touch, earth, water, fire, and air, as well as all other phenomena. So the appearances themselves are rising from the luminosity of consciousness.

Whence do these appearances arise? From the space of consciousness.

The appearances arise, and then out of habituation we identify familiar objects. I've seen a lot of people in the past who look a lot like Jane, who have a head, two legs, and so on—I am able to identify Jane as "human being, female." I had her bracketed as soon as I met her because I'd seen the likes of her before. We might say that for this tapestry of experience the space of the mind is the substantial cause—the "yarn" of appearances—and the mind that designates objects is the cooperative condition, the "weaver" that is weaving them. That's the grasping, and it may be innocuous, as in the simple designation, "There's Jane."

Hence, objects arise (1) in dependence upon prior causes and conditions. They arise (2) in dependence upon their own qualities or attributes. Were the qualities missing, the object would not appear. Last, they arise (3) by the power of conceptual designation. If you take away the object's causes, it's not there. If you take away the attributes, it's not there. If you take away the conceptual designation, there's no object that *has* the qualities we attribute to it.

To extend our understanding of this, let us delve more deeply into bases of designation. Suppose we were to cast our glance at Mount Everest, whose image, whose visual attributes, we are familiar with. Looking up at Mount Everest, we have a strong sense that of course there's really something over there and that the mountain really exists from its own side. Fine. Next, as a thought experiment, take away all those attributes by which we identify Mount Everest—its distinctive peak, the massive walls of snow and ice below, its height, location, contours, and so forth. What happened to Mount Everest? It becomes obvious that the particular mountain that has those attributes is something designated by the mind because now it is nowhere to be found. The fact that it has "this" and doesn't have "that"—the demarcations of Mount Everest as opposed to the adjacent valleys and mountains—is arbitrary. There is nothing from the side of the object that says, "I begin here and I stop there." So it is the power of conceptual designation that demarcates Mount Everest from that around it which is not Mount Everest and then allows for Mount Everest to *have* various features. Without conceptual designation Mount Everest does not exist. It exists as soon as it is designated. It stops existing as soon as it is no longer designated as such.

Taking this a little further, *who are we* before we set out taking the mind as our path? What is the mind—the vehicle, the vessel with which we are to go from here to the ground of the mind, to achieve shamatha, and use that accomplishment as a basis for future explorations? Again using Jane as an example, as I look her over, I see her body, but that is not Jane; that's only a chunk of flesh. That body is a basis of designation, but it is not Jane. Then I might hear Jane's voice on the telephone and say, "Oh, that's Jane," using her voice as the basis of designation, but this too is not Jane. Now suppose Jane were alone in a sensory deprivation tank. She is deprived of the five sensory modalities of her physical sensations. It is pitch dark, completely silent, there is no motion, and she has no clear-cut sense of her body. While in that tank thoughts, memories, images, and so forth are arising in Jane's mind. She says to herself, "Here I am. I must be here." An image of her face comes to mind. Still none of these arising mental phenomena are Jane.

Body, speech, and mind are often the bases of designation of a person. Jane could be standing in the bathroom, looking into the mirror, and thinking "Here I am," and could designate herself on the basis of her body, speech, and/or mind. Any one will do. But none of these three or any combination of them is Jane. Nonetheless, using the body, speech, and/or mind *is* a valid, conventional basis on which to say "Jane's there."

As another example, the mind is designated upon the basis of anything that arises within it. Even so, no single thing that arises, no event that arises in the space of Jane's mind—an emotion, an image, a thought—none of those are Jane's mind either, any more than any particular cell in your hand is a hand. Nevertheless, upon the basis of the collections of cells in your hand, the hand can be designated. I could just stick my pinky through a doorway, and you would say, "Oh, that's Alan's hand." You don't need to see all of the hand. Otherwise you'd never be able to designate the hand, because you *never* see all of it. You see only the front side and I see only the back side. So likewise, upon the basis of things that are not the mind—a thought, an image, consciousness, mental events—you designate your mind. None of them are your mind. Likewise with Jane, by way of body, speech, or mind—none of which are Jane—we can validly designate Jane, and that Jane we have designated can perform and experience all kinds of things.

Now let's place Jane totally out of contact with her body. It could be in the after-death bardo, where there is no physical body, or she could be in deep sleep, or in the dream state. In the dream state you are really out of touch with the body, meaning that you don't have any kind of conscious experience of it. So let's set aside the body, and let's set aside Jane's speech. We will even set aside Jane's mind, remembering that we have defined "mind" as pertaining to the matrix of mental events that arises in dependence upon the substrate consciousness, influenced by a myriad of factors from the body, environment, and so on. We have gone down to the ground, to the substrate consciousness, where Jane has lost her mind. The mind is dormant. There's only the substrate consciousness, which carries on from lifetime to lifetime, has no beginning and no end, and manifests like magic as all types of forms and all kinds of minds.

Is the substrate consciousness a person? No. It's a continuum of consciousness. But let's suppose that Jane is here, reading this or receiving these teachings. For me to turn to her and say, "You are here now because of karma you accumulated in past lives" could be a conventionally valid statement. When I ask her, what is the basis of that first "you"? Jane, the person who lives now didn't exist in past lives. Maybe she is now fifty years old. She didn't exist a hundred years ago. In my statement, "You are here now because of karma *you* accumulated in past lives," the basis of designation for the second "you" is her substrate consciousness. That's the connection between her existence now and her past lives.

Moreover, if in another lifetime she was "Billy Bob"—that was a different person. In that case I couldn't say "you," because he is not that you. Billy Bob has his own body, speech, and mind, each of which could serve as the basis of designation for him, but he shares the same continuum of the substrate consciousness as Jane. The substrate consciousness is not a person, but upon the basis of that continuum of mental consciousness, it is perfectly valid to say, "You are here because of karma *you* accumulated in past lives."

Similarly, I may say, "If you continue to practice, you will, in this or in some future life, become a buddha." The basis of designation is not necessarily your present body, especially not if I say "in some future life." By then you will have lost this body. It will have become bones, earth, dust. It has nothing to do with you in some future lifetime. It is limited within the context of a single human life within the broader context of samsara.

Now let's take a much wider view, broadened out to the vision of Dzogchen. From that perspective we can say: Jane, it is valid for you right now to say, "I am a buddha." What's the basis of designation in this case? Unless you are a buddha, it would be ridiculous to designate yourself as a buddha on the basis of your ordinary body, speech, or mind. That's not valid in any sense of the term. Likewise, on the basis of your substrate consciousness, which carries on from countless past lifetimes, to say that you are a buddha is false as well. Upon that basis you can say that you are a sentient being. However, upon the basis of the dharmakaya, which is always present, upon the basis of rigpa, which is always present, upon *that* basis of designation, which after all is not a person either, you can designate an I, saying, "I am a buddha." That is valid. Each case has a different basis of designation. None of those bases of designation are persons. But to impute a person on any one of those three is perfectly valid. It's not valid, however, to mix them up.

Is conceptual designation our exclusive gateway to knowledge? For us as ordinary beings, that which enables us to identify anything is the power of conceptual designation. For us, presently, the "unmediated realization of emptiness" may be beyond imagination. Still, there are ways of knowing that do not entail conceptual designation. Does that mean that when you've become an arya—abiding in meditative equipoise, realizing emptiness nonconceptually—since your whole conceptual apparatus is completely dormant, you don't know anything? You do know, but you know nonconceptually, in an unimaginable way, an unprecedented way, where there's a knowing arising from a nondual awareness of what you know. From that perspective there's no sense of a subject or an object, for you have transcended the dichotomy of subject and object.

Let us suppose you are an arya and you've told me you are about to slip into a nonconceptual realization of emptiness. Next, I tell some other person that you are now realizing emptiness. This is valid discourse from my perspective. From your perspective in the nonconceptual realization of emptiness, however, this means nothing at all, because you are completely out of the loop of conceptual designation and language. Just as the nonconceptual realization of emptiness does not entail conceptual designation or identification, because conceptualization is not happening, the same is true for rigpa. We hear Dzogchen teachings—all of them aimed at a nondual realization of that which is ineffable and inconceivable. Our text, the *Vajra Essence*, is one of countless books designed to help us gain that realization. We hear about rigpa and gain a conceptual understanding of it. The teachings themselves are a bridge that first of all provides us with some pointers of where to attend and how to attend. Then, just as in the process of realizing emptiness, when the conceptual veils become thinner and thinner and are then gone, the same occurs with rigpa. The language is there, the teachings are there, the pointing-out instructions are there to give us a glimpse. We then follow that taste and slowly shrug off our conceptual veils and processes of conceptual identification.

Recall this phrase from the root text, which we examined near the beginning of this chapter: "When the body and mind separate, experiences of joy and sorrow—reaching up to the state of enlightenment or down to the three realms of samsara—are all due to the mental consciousness delusively engaging with objects." When I translated that, I thought, "What? Reaching up to enlightenment?" This accomplishment, enlightenment, is all due to mental consciousness *delusively* engaging with objects? It doesn't seem to make any sense. Gyatrul Rinpoche offers this comment: "Although one does not reach the state of buddhahood by the mind deludedly engaging with objects, since awareness is primordially pure, your awareness right now is primordially pure; the sense that it reaches a state of enlightenment is due solely to one's mental constructs." Therefore, the whole notion of progressing along the path and eventually achieving enlightenment makes sense only within the context of a mind deludedly engaging with conceptual constructs. From one angle it may seem ironic, but it makes perfect sense that the deluded, impure, conventional mind plays an important, positive role in leading you on the path to enlightenment. What is it after all that reminds you to practice?

THE FRUITS OF PRACTICE

> "By taking the mind itself as the path, a person of superior faculties directly actualizes the nature of existence of suchness—ultimate reality—and realizes the consummation of samsara and nirvana, achieving liberation in the absolute domain of pristine space. A person of average faculties achieves certainty in the formless realm, and a person of inferior faculties experiences joy in the form realm. For a person of the lowest faculties, the path is experienced as happiness in the desire realm. Please, Teacher, explain how this happens."

Now we return to the initial theme of this chapter—taking the mind as the path. How remarkable. It's as if we are not even practicing "Buddhism." We are not picking up something exotic from some tradition outside of ourselves—from the "mysterious Orient," from "ancient wisdom of the East," or from the Buddhist tradition versus the Hindu or the Sufi tradition. Of course in a way we are, but essentially we are just taking *reality* as our path; and the reality that is initially most pertinent to fathoming the nature of awareness is our own minds. After all, we don't have immediate access to emptiness or rigpa. The closest access we have to these deeper truths right now is the mind. So we take that which is the closest thing we have to pristine awareness and make that our vehicle. That is taking reality as the path. In this way we can proceed with enormous assurance. We may have doubts about Buddhism and its reference to such things as Mount Meru, hungry ghosts, or cold and hot hells. We can have many qualms, as in what to take literally or metaphorically, absolutely or conventionally. For now, though, we're just taking the mind as the path. That's pretty firm ground.

Who is "a person of superior faculties?" Recall that we all have the same buddha nature. Our differences lie in our karmic backgrounds—practice from previous lifetimes and practice in this lifetime. For the time being only, that provides some people with what we call, relatively speaking, "superior faculties," others with "medium faculties," and so on. Nonetheless a person who has medium faculties at the age of twenty-two may very well have superior faculties at age fifty-two. Chances are, sooner or later, if you are moving along the path, that is exactly what's going to happen. So let's not reify these demarcations of people of different faculties.

"By taking the mind itself as the path, a person of superior faculties directly actualizes the nature of existence of suchness—ultimate reality . . ." It becomes manifest, totally real. It becomes your reality. Here *suchness* is really a synonym for emptiness. *Ultimate reality* as well, generally speaking, is a synonym for emptiness. For a person of very sharp faculties who has taken this text and studied and meditated on it well, this section alone could be enough to realize emptiness. This could be sufficient, without ever reading the vipashyana section of the *Vajra Essence* or the material we will explore below, covering the next several pages of the root text.

That material is explicitly for shamatha—but a very specific type of shamatha. Here you do not focus on an image of the Buddha or on the breath. Taking the mind as the path is something very special. Therefore it is possible that a person taking this approach, a person of superior faculties, someone very ripe, or as the Buddha said, "with very little dust on the eyes," could realize emptiness. For such a person, study and meditation of the first 9 percent of the text may be sufficient for achieving liberation.

This possibility is reminiscent of Padmasambhava's comment in *Natural Liberation*[22] where he teaches shamatha without signs. It consists of only a few paragraphs, but it is utterly simple, leading you to probe the nature of awareness, relax, and then probe again. He too says that this may be enough to realize rigpa. The approach is expressly designed for shamatha, but for a person of sharp faculties, just that modest shamatha technique may be enough to fathom rigpa. Once you've fathomed rigpa, you've fathomed the ground awareness—dharmakaya—meaning that from then on you can just take *that* as your path, putting yourself on a fast track to enlightenment. So that could mean "shamatha, and then enlightenment"—shamatha to Dzogchen to enlightenment. A superior person could bypass vipashyana as a separate series of techniques. We will all have that capacity sooner or later. The "consummation of samsara and nirvana" is the realization of the "one taste" of the whole of reality, which is none other than the nonduality of the absolute space of phenomena and primordial consciousness. It is through such realization that you achieve liberation in the absolute domain of pristine space.

In the meantime, "A person of average faculties achieves certainty," actualization, "in the formless realm." This is clearly in reference to samadhi. The formless realm lies within samsara, but this is a very subtle dimension of existence, and one that can be helpful for gaining insight into the nature of the mind. A person with average faculties fathoms a formless dimension of reality, whereas the person with superior faculties has penetrated through the three realms of existence to emptiness and has plumbed the ultimate nature of the mind, reaching beyond samsara. The person of average or ordinary faculties, within the context of samsara, fathoms the deepest levels of the dualistic mind, and "a person of inferior faculties experiences joy in the form realm." Notice he didn't say joy in the formless realm. There is no joy in the formless realm. You can achieve certainty there, but it is beyond joy and sorrow. So in the formless realm there is no joy, no bliss, and certainly no pain. It's too calm for joy or bliss. But a person of inferior faculties does experience joy in the form realm. This can be achieved by way of shamatha. Shamatha provides you with access to the form realm. It crosses that threshold to the experience of bliss.

"For a person of the lowest faculties, the path is experienced as happiness in the desire realm." That is, you may not for the time being achieve shamatha; you're still in the desire realm. But by following this path you can acquire a great sense of well-being, one that is more robust than the happiness we normally experience as ordinary beings, because that tends to be almost entirely stimulus driven. Usually we feel pleasure due to an event such as a pleasant sensory experience, a happy thought, a beautiful visualization; we receive a kind word, taste good food, have good sex, recall a pleasant memory, or get a really good night's sleep. Something happens to the mind, either mentally or by way of the senses, internally or externally. Some object comes in, arouses us, and we feel pleasure. Then when the object leaves, the stimulus vanishes and the happiness is gone. Normally, for ordinary sentient beings mucking about in samsara, that's how pleasure operates.

Now, however, we are stepping out of that syndrome because we are

balancing the mind, cultivating equilibrium of the attention, of the emotions, of our cognition. Developing greater sanity, we experience more
and more frequently a sense of well-being unrelated to any external cata-
lyst, one that arises directly from the mind's nature. In the face of neutral
stimuli, we discover we nonetheless feel pretty good. This is not because
these neutral stimuli somehow improved. It is because the mind that appre-
hends them is much more healthy. It's a very simple thing—the mind is less
afflicted. Within the mundane context you are achieving greater psychological balance—that's sanity.

Once you've achieved shamatha you've gotten a mind, instead of your
mind having you. Now your mind, for the first time, is not dysfunctional.
It is now serviceable. You can do with that mind what you wish, and that
feels very, very good. Even in between meditation sessions, as long as you
don't lose your shamatha, there is an ongoing sense of well-being. Then
when you enter into meditation you experience bliss. Just call it up whenever you like. Hence you can see why mental afflictions would arise so
rarely and so weakly under these conditions.

5

THE EXPLICIT INSTRUCTIONS

I n asking the Teacher to "explain how this happens," Great Boundless Emptiness wants him to cut to the chase, to explain how you can attain a deeper understanding of shamatha—"Please explain, how to take the mind as your path." As we shall see in the next few pages of the text, this simple practice gives rise to a wide variety of results depending on the qualities of the mind, in other words, the degree of spiritual maturation that you bring to practice. The results are all quite good—happiness within the desire realm. I could go for that!

> He replied, "O Vajra of Mind, first merge this mind with external space and remain in meditative equipoise for seven days. Then fix your attention on a stone, a stick, a physical representation of the Buddha, or a letter, and remain in meditative equipoise for seven days. Then imagine a clear, radiant, five-colored *bindu* at your heart, fix your attention on it, and remain in meditative equipoise for seven days. For some, this places the mind in a state of bliss, luminosity, and vacuity. This experience, devoid of thought, like an ocean unmoved by waves, is called quiescence with signs.

The Bhagavan replied, "O Vajra of Mind, first merge this mind with external space and remain in meditative equipoise for seven days." Beginning with this sentence we encounter the explicit shamatha instructions. How do you take the mind as your path? Go off for a week and practice merging your mind with space. Find an appropriate setting, sit in the vastness of space attending to it, and remain there with your eyes open—very important, your eyes open—and simply maintain presence in space. That's all. You needn't do more. Just be present with space, the space intervening between appearing visual objects and the sense of your own subjective presence, for seven days as continuously as possible. Of course, over those seven days your sessions will probably alternate with post-sessions where you are not explicitly practicing. Generally speaking that's what yogis do; that's how to practice. However, if you had few distractions and demands on your time, you could dwell in that spaciousness continuously. Even when you are eating you can maintain that. When you're going to the bathroom, just dwell in space. That's the instruction: All day for seven days simply rest your mind in space.

What is the best environment for this practice? Clearly, sitting outside in a spacious, natural setting—for example in the mountains, the desert, or by the ocean—would be very supportive, but that is not mandatory. Whether you are in the mountains or in a small room, it is important to keep your eyes open and not grasp, not become attached to the phenomena that appear to your visual perception. So gaze into the space in front of you and notice that there is no big deal here; let this be utterly ordinary. Don't think you are doing anything special, because you are not. There's the space in front of you. Just be present with it, that is, attend to it, notice it. Avoid involving yourself with details, such as labeling: "There's a cushion. It's on a red rug. The cushion is soft. The rug is hard." If you slip into grasping like that, you've diminished the spaciousness of your meditation. You make your space rather small. You don't have to deal with those objects right now. They're not pertinent to your meditation, which means you can just ignore them.

Whatever the setting, first of all direct your awareness to the space between those objects and yourself. Then release any grasping. Set aside all conceptual designation. Be satisfied with the mere appearances arising to visual perception—shapes, patches of color. Now relax your gaze even further, looking right through intervening objects, and allow your eyes to gaze into infinity. So now, whatever objects may be there, they're out of focus

and you don't care about them. The eyes are released as if you were looking up into the sky. You are no longer attending to the intervening space
between objects out there and yourself, whether they are six feet away or
sixty miles distant. You are merging the mind with space. Space is unimpeded because colors don't impede space any more than a rainbow does.
The colors don't blot out the sky. So that gives you a big space, even if you
are practicing in a tiny room.

There is a general rule of thumb when internal distractions arise in your
meditation: Should your mind become excited, cast your gaze downward.
If the mind loses energy or clarity—becomes dull, lax—then elevate your
gaze. This advice also applies to visualization, as when you visualize a deity.
In that case, when you feel dull you raise the imagined image, and when
excitement disturbs your tranquility you lower it.

"Then fix your attention on a stone, a stick, a physical representation of
the Buddha, or a letter..." What the Tibetans mean by a letter is a syllable,
like *ah*, because all of their letters are syllables. So you can fix your attention
on a visual image of the letter, "and remain in meditative equipoise for seven
days." Choose one of those objects, any one of those, or you could shift
around a bit using several. You can choose flowers, sticks and stones, representations of the Buddha, or you can write out a Sanskrit syllable, like *om*,
ah, or *hum*, and use that or, if you wish, focus on a sacred image such as
Tara or Padmasambhava.

This is a visual practice. Although you cannot *achieve* shamatha by gazing at a visual object, this is a good way, in the initial phases of shamatha,
to stabilize your attention. You will use other techniques later. So if you are
still in the early stages of shamatha you might want to try this out. Choose
something you would enjoy looking at for twenty-four minutes. Twenty-
four-minute periods, or *ghatikas*, are recommended when you are just starting out in meditation. Just gaze at it, naturally, settling your attention on it
with the same qualities that I have been emphasizing—relaxation, stability,
and vigilance—without relinquishing any one of those three. When dis-
cursive thoughts arise, let them go and return not only your visual gaze but
your attention, your mental awareness, to the object. Continue like that
for a week.

"Then imagine a clear, radiant, five-colored *bindu* at your heart"—*bindu* means an orb, a little sphere—"fix your attention on it, and remain in meditative equipoise for seven days." For the *bindu*, if you can imagine one quite small, that's great, but the size of a pea would be sufficient—something fairly small and round. It's glistening with five colors—white, yellow, red, green, and blue—as if it were a prism, glowing from within. The five colors are symbolic, relating to the different vital energies. Don't forget to keep your eyes open.

"For some, this places the mind in a state of bliss, luminosity, and vacuity." That means for some—people of superior faculties—seven days times these three practices will lead you to realization of shamatha, or quiescence—a state of bliss, luminosity, and nonconceptuality. "This experience, devoid of thought, like an ocean unmoved by waves, is called *quiescence with signs*." Quiescence is shamatha. A sign is an object of the mind that can be identified within a conceptual framework. External space is a sign, because you're looking at it, and it is "this" as opposed to "that." So it is one object among myriad objects. Even though external space is not an object in the gross sense, it is an object of the mind that can be identified within a conceptual framework. So that is one kind of sign. Then the next ones are easy: a stone, a stick, and a physical representation of the Buddha are obviously signs. A sign can be internal too, purely in the domain of the mind, such as the visualized orb of light. Anything that you can mentally point to and identify, whether it is in the mind or out in external space, is a sign.

As suggested above, it is possible, if you are a person with very sharp faculties, to achieve shamatha in the first seven days, or in the second seven, or in the third. If so, you can move right on to the next stage, vipashyana. The reason for doing preliminary practices is to be able to so prime the pump that you can move through shamatha with relatively few cuts and bruises. So you may achieve quiescence with signs with any one of those three techniques or with a combination of them.

But if you do not achieve shamatha after those twenty-one days—how come?

PSYCHOPHYSICAL OBSTRUCTIONS

"Some cannot calm their thoughts because the mind is so agitated, and they experience uncomfortable pains and maladies in the heart, the life-force channel, and so on. Those with unstable minds, with a wind constitution, or with coarse minds may fall unconscious or slip into a trance. Such people should relax and let thoughts be as they are, continually observing them with unwavering mindfulness and careful introspection.

The life-force channel is the central channel that goes right through the heart chakra. Among those practices, the one that's most likely to give you trouble, based on many people's experience, is visualizing a *bindu* at your heart. You bring *prana*, or vital energy, to the region where you direct your mind. If you bring a coarse, afflicted mind, and then you concentrate it tightly and put it right in your heart chakra and do that for seven days, for many hours a day, you can create an imbalance in the flow of energies at your heart—a condition called *soglung*. *Soglung* is the life-supporting energy (*lung*), or *prana*, that's located in the heart chakra. Everyone has it. But when Tibetans say, "You have soglung," they mean you have an imbalance of soglung. You have disrupted this life-sustaining energy at your heart chakra.

What are the consequences of such an imbalance? Of course we are not functioning well to begin with. That's why our minds are dysfunctional and our *prana* systems are out of balance; and that is why it is important to practice shamatha. When our mind is further out of whack, exceptionally out of balance, then we experience symptoms such as feelings of heaviness, darkness, sadness, and fear, all located around the heart. You'll feel an overall tightness, similar to the feeling of your face when it is wearing a mask; it gets very tight. You may feel emotionally fragile, as if you might burst into tears at any moment. You may have a general sense of anxiety, feeling ill at ease. You can have insomnia or indigestion, because you're so "heavy." It's almost as if you're walking around with a lot of dead weight. We Westerners would encapsulate these as symptoms of a "nervous breakdown" or "clinical depression." Tibetans call it disruption or imbalance of the life-sustaining energy at the heart. This is something to avoid.

One common way of getting this soglung imbalance is by bearing down really hard in shamatha practice—throwing relaxation to the wind. You say "Enlightenment or bust!" and try to do it with sheer grit. That's the way to really throw your system out of whack. So note the early symptoms. If they are recurrent—not just the occasional pangs that are normal when you have a bad day—and you see that it seems to be related to your meditation, stop meditating and check with the teacher. Or go surfing, or see some really fun movies. Lighten up, enjoy your life, enjoy friends, music, a good meal, go to a nice spacious environment. Do not continue meditating in a forced manner. You'll do yourself damage, and that damage can linger. So if you do the visualization practice of the *bindu* at the heart, do so with a balanced, relaxed, happy mind. If you want to visualize there but are unsure about it, do it for short periods. This is important advice.

When he speaks of "those with unstable minds, with a wind constitution," as far as we are concerned the author may be referring to those of us who live in modern cities because, culturally speaking, we have very unstable minds. We drive at seventy miles an hour on the freeway, we eat on the run, we do all sorts of things that people in rural Tibet a hundred years ago couldn't even imagine doing. When the Tibetan doctor Lobsang Rapgay came here and examined the pulses of Westerners (the pulse is the principal diagnostic tool of Tibetan medicine), he found we were all suffering from wind disorders. From the Tibetan medical viewpoint our whole civilization has this malady. You may be comforted with his comment, "Considering how ill you all are, you're coping extraordinarily well."

Within a threefold scheme basic to Tibetan medicine—wind, bile, phlegm—the wind constitution is associated with the air element. People dominated by the wind element tend to speak very quickly and usually have light bodies and very angular features. They're light on their feet. They love to laugh, they're gregarious, and everything is fast. Their minds are always churning.

So *we* are "those with unstable minds, with a wind constitution, or with coarse minds." Just look at the kind of entertainments we prefer and our general lifestyle. We are bombarded with very gross stimuli. The content needn't be crude or barbaric, but we are bombarded with a lot of very coarse sensations—traffic noise, blaring televisions, jet airplanes overhead. Compare that with the youth of my teacher Geshe Rabten. Every summer he went up into the highlands above his home in eastern Tibet, spending all day every day shepherding yaks and other livestock. That was his summer job when he was a youngster. For entertainment he brought along a flute. Now think of what your average American sixteen-year-old does.

The traditional Tibetan lifestyle is relatively subtle; the accepted lifestyle of modernity is coarse. In the Tibetan case, when you have all that spaciousness and so few things happening within it, you are bound to attend to what is occurring. Since the things that are happening are relatively subtle, the mind that attends to them becomes subtle. On the other hand, when you go to a movie with digital Dolby sound—with the volume very loud—and all the other stuff we have here in the West, this is relatively coarse. That's the norm for us. So I would say that generally speaking many of us have coarse minds. With that phrase the author seems to have hit the mark for people living in the modern world. With our coarse minds, if we were to go off for seven days and focus on a *bindu* at the heart, we might very well "fall unconscious or slip into a trance."

For those who have stable minds, balanced constitutions, subtle minds, focusing on the *bindu* could take them all the way to shamatha. It will be very deep shamatha, because they will be drawing all that energy into their heart chakra, into a very small point, with five colors. It will serve them extremely well. But for many modern practitioners, that will not be an appropriate technique.

Those with coarse minds "should relax and let thoughts be as they are, continually observing them with unwavering mindfulness and careful introspection." Notice the emphasis on "should relax." He places it first. Because many of us are so wound up, the first step is to relax. Our minds are so stressed out, cluttered, and unstable—so just relax. Let your awareness be spacious and quiet. If you wish to achieve shamatha, but your mind is habitually unstable and cluttered with thoughts, your practice is going to be immensely frustrating. You want something you are not getting—that's the nature of frustration. Frustration ties you in knots. It makes you tight, constricted, unhappy, emotionally unbalanced—not a good platform for shamatha.

Does that mean that we normal, mentally hyper Westerners have no chance at enlightenment? Should we back away from Dharma practice and just have fun and pray that we'll be reborn in a pure realm? No! There is one technique that opens the door. And if we can get through that door, we can move on to Dzogchen. Here it is again: Relax. "Relax and let thoughts be as they are," which does not mean you have a preference for *no thoughts*. Memorize it. You do not need to suppress thoughts (trying to do so will, of course, lead to frustration). *Let thoughts be as they are*. This means you're not intruding on them. You're not trying to force them to shut up. You're not even trying to create space around them or make them less dense. You're not trying to do anything to the thoughts at all. "Relax and let thoughts be as they are."

What is the difference between that approach and just "spacing out," sitting there with perpetually wandering thoughts? The answer is in our text: it is to be "continually observing them." You allow any and all thoughts to arise—nasty thoughts, happy thoughts, long thoughts, short thoughts, gross thoughts, subtle thoughts, imagery, emotions—everything. Be completely uninhibited, letting thoughts arise in free association. The nastiest thought you ever had in your whole life—if that's what comes up, that one's just as good as the thought of taking refuge in the Three Jewels. "Let thoughts be as they are." But rather than just spacing out, letting them spin endlessly, you observe them continuously. Düdjom Lingpa knows perfectly well that you're not going to do this flawlessly, so you just do your best, "continually observing them with unwavering mindfulness and careful introspection," which means that with the faculty of introspection, you are monitoring the quality of your mindfulness.

The normal habit of getting caught in distracting thoughts, or rumination, is what I call an obsessive-compulsive delusional disorder. Thoughts arise obsessively, even if we want them to calm down. We are compulsively abducted by them, with our attention being riveted on their referents, with the mind wandering aimlessly through the three times and the ten direc-

BUSINESS REPLY MAIL
FIRST-CLASS MAIL   PERMIT NO. 1100   SOMERVILLE, MA

POSTAGE WILL BE PAID BY ADDRESSEE

WISDOM PUBLICATIONS
199 ELM ST
SOMERVILLE MA   02144-9908

Wisdom

WISDOM PUBLICATIONS

Please fill out and return this card if you would like to receive our catalogue and special offers. The postage is already paid!

NAME

ADDRESS

CITY / STATE / ZIP / COUNTRY

EMAIL

Sign up for our newsletter and special offers at wisdompubs.org

Wisdom Publications is a non-profit charitable organization.

tions. And we deludedly regard our thoughts as being clear and accurate representations of reality. We tend to think our thoughts represent the whole truth about whatever it is we're thinking about, but that's never true. At best, thoughts capture just a fragment of truth, and at worst they consist of pure fictions that we take to be reality.

Each time we get caught up in such ruminations it's as if we were reborn in a microcosm of samsara. We were unaware when we first fell into this chain of thoughts, and while we're immersed in such thinking without being aware of it, we are carried along by our past habits of craving and aversion. Every night a similar pattern occurs when we enter into a nonlucid dream—dreaming without being aware that we are dreaming. We were unaware when the dream first began, and while we're immersed in this microcosm of samsara—obsessed, compulsive, and delusional—we are propelled from one dream situation to another by the forces of craving and hostility.

This practice of taking the mind as the path is a method for becoming lucid during the waking state with respect to the flow of thoughts. We recognize them for what they are—like becoming lucid in a dream—and in so doing, we break the chain of obsessions, compulsion, and delusion. Here is a direct path to freedom, which leads to greater and greater freedom both while awake and while asleep, and this freedom may lead to the infinitely greater freedom from samsara as a whole.

> "Stillness without thinking of anything is called stillness in the domain of the essential nature of the mind. The movements and appearances of various thoughts are called fluctuations. Not letting any thoughts go by unnoticed, but recognizing them with mindfulness and introspection, is called awareness. With that explanation, come to know these points.

Here "essential nature" refers to the conventional nature; we are not speaking of the ultimate nature. As for the movements and appearances of various thoughts being called "fluctuations," there are interesting parallels to mainstream physics here. According to one modern theory the vacuum of space contains fluctuations—mass/energy is thought to consist of fluctuations of empty space itself. Similarly here, thoughts, emotions—all the contents of the mind—have no existence apart from the substrate consciousness. They're not envisioned as separate phenomena that have somehow wandered into the space of the mind. The appearances to the mind are nothing other than fluctuations of that space. They are space—"the vacuum"—taking on form.

Recognizing thoughts "with mindfulness and introspection is called awareness," but this is not rigpa. This is just simple, straightforward "being aware." "With that explanation, come to know these points." We now receive practice instructions.

SETTLING THE MIND IN ITS NATURAL STATE

> "'Now to remain for a long time in the domain of the essential nature of the mind, I shall be watchful, observing motion, keeping my body straight, and maintaining vigilant mindfulness.' When you say this and practice it, fluctuating thoughts do not cease; however, without getting lost in them as usual, mindful awareness exposes them. By applying yourself to this practice continuously at all times, both during and between meditation sessions, eventually all coarse and subtle thoughts will be calmed in the empty expanse of the essential nature of your mind. You will become still, in an unfluctuating state in which you experience bliss like the warmth of a fire, luminosity like the dawn, and nonconceptuality like an ocean unmoved by waves. Yearning for this and believing in it, you will not be able to bear being separated from it, and you will hold fast to it.

In order to "remain for a long time in the domain of the essential nature of the mind," I must be "watchful, observing motion, keeping my body straight, and maintaining vigilant mindfulness." Notice it says to keep the body straight. It does not say that it must be erect. Practicing in this way, "eventually all coarse and subtle thoughts will be calmed in the empty expanse of the essential nature of your mind." This happens because you are watching the thoughts, maintaining vigilant mindfulness, without either getting carried away by them or latching on to them. In a word, you are not grasping. You cannot be carried away by thoughts if you are not grasping on to them, nor can you identify with thoughts without grasping on to them. This speaks volumes about the nature of the mind and its perturbations, or fluctuations. So, by observing without distraction, without grasping—by just allowing mental processes to arise and pass of their own accord—over time the coarse and subtle thoughts dissolve, dissipate into the space of the mind, and you settle into the ground of the mind, the substrate consciousness. There is no clever technique involved here. On the contrary, by not engaging with them, thoughts will usually, over time, thin out. They lose their power over you and become fainter and fainter. If you don't grasp, the mind will self-heal and dissolve into its ground.

What happens when all these coarse and subtle thoughts are calmed in the empty expanse of the essential nature of your mind? "You will become still, in an unfluctuating state in which you will experience bliss like the warmth of a fire, luminosity like the dawn, and nonconceptuality like an ocean unmoved by waves." That is a description, in one sentence, of dwelling luminously in the substrate consciousness after having achieved shamatha. The next sentence—"Yearning for this and believing in it, you will not be able to bear being separated from it, and you will hold fast to it"—describes a virtual intoxication with shamatha. Not knowing any better, you might take that as your goal, holding fast to it and saying, "Hallelujah, I'm home free for the rest of my life; I can turn on those three qualities with a switch. No matter what happens to me, I've got my little escape capsule." It's very tempting to believe that.

By itself, however, shamatha leads nowhere. There's no liberation here. There's no irreversible transformation. You just put a pause on samsara—call "Time out!"—and dwell in this ethically neutral ground. Eventually the power of your samadhi will dissipate, and you will be right back among the gang of samsaric wanderers. Düdjom Lingpa is saying that once you have achieved such an exalted state, it will be very hard not to hold fast to it. You will strongly wish to remain there.

> "If you get caught up in bliss, this will cast you into the desire realm; if you get caught up in luminosity, this will propel you into the form realm; and if you get caught up in nonconceptuality, this will launch you to the peak of mundane existence. Therefore, understand that while these are indispensable signs of progress for individuals entering the path, it is a mistake to get caught up in them indefinitely.

Three qualities that you will be able to identify distinctly—bliss, luminosity, and nonconceptuality—will manifest in you. Bear in mind that you can grasp on not only to the objects of the mind but also to states of mind. Now we are looking at the big picture. What happens if, having achieved shamatha, and drawing forth the bliss of the substrate consciousness, you then latch on to it? Karmically speaking, what flows from that? You are cast back into the desire realm. Furthermore, "if you get caught up in luminosity"—the radiance, the clarity in that state—if you fix on that, "this will propel you into the form realm." If you get caught up in nonconceptuality—the sheer silence, the stillness, the lack of perturbation, the open spaciousness of it—if you cling to that—"this will launch you to the peak of mundane existence," which is to say, the formless realms. In all of these cases, you are still in samsara.

These are indeed "indispensable signs of progress"—you cannot proceed without them. On the one hand, without shamatha you will not go beyond cycling in samsara. You do need to experience the substrate consciousness with these three qualities. Yet, having experienced them, if you cling to any one of them, you are stuck. You must experience each of these three qualities, and you must learn not to grasp on to them. You should not take the attitude, "Well, since I would surely grasp on to them if I had them, I will avoid them." Thinking along these lines is like getting stuck in preschool.

So, since these are "indispensable signs of progress for individuals entering the path," you enter into shamatha, and once you achieve it you can savor it for a while. Hang out there for a few hours, a few days, maybe a few weeks. Enjoy it. It is said that when the Buddha Shakyamuni achieved enlightenment, he lingered there for forty-nine days under the bodhi tree. He didn't immediately walk to Sarnath and begin teaching. For a while he simply took in his enlightenment. Remember, achieving shamatha is a faint facsimile of attaining enlightenment. So when you do achieve shamatha, take some time to enjoy it. "Bliss like the warmth of a fire, luminosity like the dawn, nonconceptuality like an ocean unmoved by waves"—enjoy it, but don't become so enamored of it that you fall into the extreme of quietude.

> "That is called ordinary quiescence of the path, and if you achieve stability in it for a long time, you will have achieved the critical feature of stability in your mindstream. However, know that among unrefined people in this degenerate era, very few appear to achieve more than fleeting stability. Nowadays, deities appear to some people, who settle their attention on them. To some, visions of buddhafields appear, and they stabilize and settle their minds on these. Some especially experience bliss, luminosity, or nonconceptuality, and they settle on this. To others, images of their guru, rainbows, light, and *bindus* appear, so they settle on these, and so forth. Understand that, due to the functioning of the channels and elements of each individual, not everyone's experience is the same."

Having achieved stability is described as a "critical feature"—once again, something indispensable. You cannot progress very far on the path without it—"the critical feature of stability in your mindstream." He notes however that "very few appear to achieve more than fleeting stability." This statement echoes what Tsongkhapa said in the fifteenth century and what Düdjom Lingpa's contemporary Mipham Rinpoche said in the nineteenth century. It is certainly true as well for the twentieth and twenty-first centuries. To illustrate, observe that there are hundreds of thousands of meditators in the United States and Europe. There are numerous Tibetan meditators inside and outside of Tibet. Many of these folks are practicing Vajrayana in the Tibetan tradition. They are meditating on bodhichitta, vipashyana, Vajrayana, Mahamudra, and Dzogchen, some of them immersing themselves in three-year retreats on the above topics. Many others engage in vipassana retreats for weeks or months on end, while others devote themselves to extensive Zen sesshins. How many of these practitioners have achieved shamatha? It's difficult to say, but since relatively few people are practicing shamatha as described here, it seems likely that relatively few people are achieving the results described here.

"Very few appear to achieve more than fleeting stability." People do a little bit of shamatha, are satisfied with that, then think, "Now let's get on with it—vipashyana. Let's do the important stuff: bodhichitta, vipashyana, stage of generation, stage of completion, and Dzogchen." That is like a musician tuning his or her instrument quickly and imperfectly and then saying, "This is boring. I can do so many more interesting things than tuning my instrument. I want to play Tchaikovsky, Brahms, Beethoven, Scott Joplin. Tuning is so boring; let's get on with the music!" I really don't think that shamatha is unbelievably hard. I think that most people are simply impatient, eager to get on with other things rather than devoting themselves to sustained, single-pointed practice to achieve exceptional levels of mental balance and focused attention.

Having said that, is it possible to achieve shamatha by way of the stage of generation? Yes, but how many actually do it? The shamatha part of the stage of generation comes when you are sitting quietly and stabilizing in pure vision and divine pride. In the Gelug tradition, in three-year retreat, you spend almost all your time doing mantras, hundreds of thousands of mantras. Will you achieve shamatha while doing a mantra? Not likely. It wasn't intended for that. It is similar in the Kagyü and Nyingma three-year retreats. There you spend a lot of time engaging in a wide variety of practices, starting with months on end devoted to the preliminary practices. During the course of the three years you will certainly engage in generation-stage practice and various completion-stage practices such as *tummo*. But how much of the time are you devoting to tuning your mind through the practice of shamatha? Not much. Yet Düdjom Lingpa has already told us twice now that shamatha is "indispensable" and "critical." So if people are settling for fleeting stability, that means they're not taking such advice very seriously.

Returning to our particular practice, what happens in the course of shamatha, especially in this form of shamatha, where clearly we are directed to free associate—to stabilize our awareness in the midst of the movements of the mind? All kinds of things appear because the approach to practice is free, unimpeded. What are some of the possibilities? "Nowadays deities appear to some people, who settle their attention on them." So they are cruising along, settling the mind in its natural state, and lo and behold, there's Manjushri, or there's Tara. They think, "Cool. I've been waiting for you for a long time." In doing so, they set up a preference. All of a sudden they are grasping. "I had a vision of Tara. I've got to tell somebody. I saw Tara! What did *you* see? You didn't see Tara? Oh, but I did!" Grasping.

Wouldn't you love to see a divine being—Buddha Shakyamuni or Tara or Manjushri or Padmasambhava? But are you going to grasp when that happens? Buddhas appear to some; and they might stabilize and settle their minds on that. In other words, they fixate on that. Do they achieve shamatha? Maybe so—maybe not. If you are grasping, though, you are not doing this practice. Certainly to grasp on to such appearances would be enormously tempting. "To some, visions of buddhafields appear, and they stabilize and settle their minds on these." Visions of buddhafields—wow! "Some especially experience bliss, luminosity, or nonconceptuality, and they settle on this." They latch right on to that. This can happen well before you achieve shamatha.

I know someone for whom bliss arises immediately when he sits down to meditate. What do you suppose he does? He really likes bliss, and since it comes to him so easily, he's on it like a hummingbird on a hummingbird feeder. He is grasping on to joy. Unfortunately, when you are doing that, you are not doing the practice. For some people it is luminosity that comes easily. For others it's nonconceptuality. In any of these cases if you grasp, you are not doing the practice. The practice is not grasping. Oh, but there's more!

"To others, images of their guru, rainbows, light, and *bindus* appear, so they settle on these, and so forth." Wouldn't it be marvelous to experience a vision of Düdjom Rinpoche? Dilgo Khyentse Rinpoche? Tsongkhapa? You name it! Images of the guru well up. How about some rainbow lights appearing, or other apparitions of light such as *bindus*? This sounds like a psychedelic experience but without drugs. Whether you grasp on to them or not, the experiences vary: "Understand that, due to the functioning of the channels and elements of each individual, not everyone's experience is the same."

NYAM—SIGNS OF MEDITATIVE EXPERIENCE

> Great Boundless Emptiness asked, "O Teacher, Bhagavan, please explain how meditative experiences arise as a result of such practice."
>
> He replied, "O Vajra of Mind, awareness is nakedly revealed in all the tantras, oral transmissions, and practical instructions of the past. Among them, I will not describe more than a mere fraction of the ways the signs of experience occur. Because individual constitutions and faculties are unimaginably complex and their array of experiences is equally unimaginable, I know that there is no uniformity among them. So understand that I will speak only in the most general terms.

The Tibetan word *nyam* is translated as "experience" or "meditative experience." He describes much later in the text that it is crucial to distinguish nyam from realization (*togpa*). There is a great difference between the two. All the things that were just described—joy, clarity, visions of buddhafields, gurus, rainbow light, *bindus*—all of those are nyam. So is a sense of depression, a general feeling of anxiety, and dread. So are bliss, paranoia, and insomnia. Nyam comprises a variety of types of anomalous, transient experiences that are catalyzed by authentic meditative practice. The experiences may be pleasant, unpleasant, frightening, euphoric, or ecstatic. They may be interesting or boring. They may be exotic or fascinating or terrifying, psychological or somatic. They are aroused by meditation, in particular by this practice mode of luminous free association—settling the mind in its natural state. These nyam, these meditative experiences—including the most glorious ones—must not be mistaken for realization.

The Teacher will describe a mere fraction of the various signs of experience that occur, because "individual constitutions and faculties are unimaginably complex." "Constitution" refers to the body's humoral formation of wind, bile, and phlegm. "Faculties" means the degree of intelligence, perceptiveness, the stability of your attention and so on—your mental faculties. Bear in mind that when you sit down to meditate, you bring with you imprints from countless past lives plus all of the complexities of this life.

The Teacher says he will speak in the most general terms. Great Boundless Emptiness is asking, "What kind of stuff happens when you do this practice?" and the Teacher responds telling him, "The variety is infinite—there is no way I can synthesize it. But I can give you a little taste of it, some generalities."

"The indeterminate, inconceivable range of experiences is inexpressible. But teachers with great experience, proficiency in the explanations of the stages and paths, and extrasensory perception, owing to the strength of their great wisdom, are knowledgeable and clear. Also, although vidyadharas from matured vidyadharas to vidyadharas with mastery over life might not have firsthand knowledge of the ways experiences occur, they know them directly by means of extrasensory perception. Even without this, they can free others from their experiences by adapting and interpreting the instructions.

The "indeterminate," i.e., unpredictable, "inconceivable," unimaginably vast, "range of experiences is inexpressible." Nevertheless, teachers with "great experience, proficiency in explanations of the stages and paths, and extrasensory perception," which implies they have achieved shamatha and vipashyana, and "owing to the strength of their great wisdom"—certainly a wisdom that arises from shamatha—"are knowledgeable and clear."

Therefore, if you've achieved shamatha you can give others experiential guidance in the practice of shamatha all the way to the culmination of this practice. Because you have thoroughly fathomed this practice and have tapped into your substrate consciousness you may have extrasensory perception, like a doctor who can make a diagnosis by directly sensing the internal state of another person's body. Similarly, with extrasensory perception you can directly access the internal state of another person's mind.

Next the text speaks of "vidyadharas," those who have gained unmediated realization of rigpa, "from matured vidyadharas to vidyadharas with mastery over life…" There are four stages of the vidyadhara state, and this refers to the first two stages. "Matured vidyadharas" are on the first stage, and on the second stage are "vidyadharas with mastery over life," so-called because they have the power to determine how long they will live. Now these vidyadharas may not have firsthand knowledge of all of these experiences, which is to say that if you are experiencing a particular nyam, it is quite possible that a vidyadhara you might consult with will not have experienced it for himself or herself already because the diversity of nyam is so vast. Even so, they do know them "directly by means of extrasensory perception." They can simply look into your mind and know what's going on. Just as an animal becomes caught in a snare and cannot move, so we can be snared in the nyam that arise in the course of this practice. In such cases vidyadharas "can free others from their experiences by adapting and interpreting the instructions." They can find the skillful means to release us, so that we students can continue along the path to exceptional sanity.

> "For example, devas, rishis, brahmins, acharyas, and so on who practice samadhi cultivate it by focusing on various seed syllables. As a result, whatever purpose these syllables had in meditation can be accomplished later by reciting them. Later by reciting the syllables for whatever illness they focus upon, they can benefit men and women. Likewise, vidyadharas can intuitively identify all illnesses; or, by revealing techniques of meditation and recitation for that purpose, they can dispel all but a few diseases that are incurable due to past karma. This being the case, it goes without saying that they can guide a yogin's experiences on the path.

The Teacher is now referring to different types of sentient beings, not only humans, but gods, rishis (contemplative adepts), brahmins (priests), and acharyas (masters). These terms are used broadly in India in various traditions, not only Buddhist. Gods in this context are nonhuman entities who are adept in samadhi. Samadhi is practiced in a wide range of religions—

by Buddhists, Hindus, Jains, and so on. Those who practice samadhi "cultivate it by focusing," for instance, "on various seed syllables," like *om*, *ah*, *hum*, *hrih*, and many others. These seed syllables are part of the mystic lore of classical India.

We find a similar notion in Christianity. The Gospel of John states that "In the beginning was the Word... and the Word became flesh." The notion of reality emerging from the *word*, of reality emerging from the syllable, a seed syllable, is quite broad culturally, suggesting that this idea must be attuned to something pretty deep. Judaism is different from Buddhism, which differs from Christianity, and that from Hinduism, and so on. And yet this idea ranges across religious boundaries. It may be the case that our realm, the desire realm, emerges from the *nimittas*, or archetypal forms, of the form realm—those quintessential symbols of earth, water, fire, air, and so on. If that were the case, by mastering the seed syllables, one might master the phenomena that emanate from them. This may be the source of spells. When there is no samadhi behind it, this is no more than a fairy tale. However, when it is empowered by samadhi, such effects may be perfectly possible.

In one treatise from traditional Tibetan medicine, there is a long section on specific mantras for curing specific illnesses. The pills used in Tibetan medicine consist of compounds of specific ingredients pertaining to earth, fire, water, air—all designed to be in balance. Likewise, a mantra is a concoction of syllables. If you've mastered these seed syllables, you can utilize them together in "compounds" to heal. Samadhi is the essential ingredient. Without that you have nothing, although faith may have some power. "As a result, whatever purpose those syllables had in meditation," the reason you chose those syllables, "can be accomplished later by reciting them." This is similar to the *nimitta*. Once you achieve the *nimitta* of the earth element you can use it later in post-meditation to "benefit men and women."

Likewise, vidyadharas—beings way beyond mere shamatha and the mastery of samadhi and certain seed syllables—"can intuitively identify all illnesses." Having tapped into rigpa, their powers of intuition are off the charts. They recognize symptoms of specific illnesses intuitively, directly from rigpa. Or, "by revealing techniques of meditation and recitation for that purpose, they can dispel all but a few diseases that are incurable due to past karma." Therefore it goes without saying that they can guide another person's experiences on the path. The power of their intuition is so enormous that they can directly perceive ordinary illnesses, and they also can detect specific afflictions that are impeding you on the path of shamatha.

> "If foolish teachers lacking any of these qualities give instruction to students and say that all these experiences will arise in the mind-stream of a single individual, they are deceiving both themselves and others, and the life force of their students will fall prey to the maras. Why? Outer disturbances such as the magical displays of gods and demons, inner disturbances including various physical illnesses, and secret disturbances of unpredictable experiences of joy and sorrow can all arise.

Now, in contrast, if foolish teachers who lack these essential qualities give students instruction and say that all of these varied experiences will occur for a single individual, "they are deceiving both themselves and others, and the life force of their students will fall prey to the maras." That is, they will fall into the mental afflictions. Such foolish teachers come along with a list of the stuff that happens through shamatha, and they assume it is true for everyone. All they do with that is sow confusion.

Why do these students fall prey to maras? There are three types of disturbances that can and very likely will crop up in the course of shamatha practice if you take it to its culmination. First he mentions "outer disturbances such as magical displays of gods and demons." The Tibetan yogi Gen Lamrimpa, at the beginning of a one-year shamatha retreat for Westerners that I organized in 1988, warned, "As you're here for one whole year, practicing shamatha many hours a day, you may very well experience some apparitions, images, or visions of demons or gods." Among the twelve people participating, at least as far as I know, not a single one reported any visions of that sort. It's just not part of our conditioning here in the West. We don't expect it. We believe in electromagnetic fields that have no material existence. We believe in photons that consist of little packets of energy, even though no one quite knows exactly what energy *is*. We don't believe in fairies, however, or earth spirits, tree spirits, or *naga* serpents, or gods. The scientific revolution took a great broom and swept demons and the like out of our universe, leaving us with quarks (some of which have "charm"), electrons (which have no spatial dimension), electromagnetic fields (which are physical but contain no matter), neutrinos (which are barely detectable), and superstrings (for which there is no empirical evidence)—not to mention dark matter and dark energy, which are complete mysteries.

Most Westerners are more likely to bump into a superstring than they are to see a demon. But if you are from a traditional society like Tibet, when outer disturbances occur you may very well be obstructed by magical displays, apparitions of gods and demons. *Our* outer disturbances are more likely to manifest as hassles from our neighbors, red ants, scorpions, and other unwelcome critters in our environment. In either case, outer disturbances are one possibility.

Then there are "inner disturbances including various physical illnesses." These may come from the outside or from inside. Not all illnesses are caused by external stimuli. They can appear because your body itself is made up of the four elements and these can fall out of harmony. Using free association to dredge the depths of your personal samsara can bring up a lot of interesting things that can manifest in some very bizarre and sometimes exceptionally unpleasant physical symptoms. Again, they are just nyam.

Then there are also "secret disturbances of unpredictable experiences of joy and sorrow." These can all arise and without warning. You look at your body and see that it's fine. You open your eyes, everything's fine. Then suddenly you are in the depths of depression for no apparent reason. You can't figure it out. Or suddenly you're just elated, overjoyed, and there's no reason that you can see. That's what's meant here by "secret": not outer, not inner, but mysterious—not easily ascertainable.

> "When giving instructions on the mind's nature, foolish, unintelligent teachers explain the causes for disturbing experiences; yet when they occur, such teachers do not recognize them as such and mistake

them for illnesses. Then they compound this by blaming these experiences on demons. They think anxieties portend death, and they
insist that their students resort to divinations, astrology, and medical
treatment. Then, if the students see the faces of demons and malevolent beings, they may turn to various rituals and other countermeasures. But whatever they do turns out to be completely
detrimental, without bringing them an iota of benefit, and finally
death is the only way out. In this way, the teacher becomes a mara
for students, as if he or she had given them a deadly poison. Ponder
this point carefully, and apply skillful means!

Here the Teacher is trying to prevent us from being misled by incompetent
teachers whose understanding is no more than theoretical. They give the
generic explanation of nyam, "yet when they occur, such teachers do not
recognize them as such and mistake them for illnesses." In other words,
they take a mundane perspective instead of considering that maybe this
imbalance is arising because you are practicing correctly. They reduce it to
an ordinary view, saying, "Oh, that's an illness."

"Then they compound this by blaming these experiences on demons."
This statement relates of course to nineteenth-century Tibet. In that context the meditating student might become ill, and the foolish teacher will
say, "It must be a demon; it's an earth spirit; it's a naga!" They believed in
such entities as much as we believe in viruses and bacteria. While most
ordinary people have never seen a virus or a bacterium, biologists have
observed them through their microscopes. Likewise, most Tibetans have
never seen demons or nagas, but highly advanced contemplatives claim to
have observed them with the power of their samadhi. Incompetent teachers blame bizarre experiences on such nonhuman beings, instead of recognizing the problem simply as a nyam and dealing with it as such.

"They think anxieties portend death." You are practicing and suddenly
you feel this nameless dread. So the foolish teacher says, "I think maybe this
portends you are going to die soon. We'd better whip out some special
long-life ceremony." "Then, if the students see the faces of demons and
malevolent beings, they may turn to various rituals and other countermea-

sures." All of these are just manifestations of your own mind, but instead of simply recognizing them for what they are, you project them onto external reality. At least within the traditional Tibetan context, you arrange for religious ceremonies, you pay some monks to recite mantras and take other countermeasures. You may wear special amulets, a special hat, perform mudras. Of course—not wanting to recognize this as simply an emanation of your mind—you go a little cuckoo.

Naturally this brings no benefit at all and is in fact detrimental. "In this way, the teacher becomes a mara for students." A sound guru is one who leads you toward enlightenment. A mara is one who leads you in the opposite direction. The teacher becomes a mara for his students because he confuses them, throws them back into samsara, "as if he or she had given them a deadly poison. Ponder this point carefully, and apply skillful means!"

In the course of a long retreat or any kind of serious practice, you may get ill on occasion. Does the advice given above imply that you should not take any medication, just have faith in Buddha? No. We are just being cautioned to be sensible. During a retreat it is sensible to maintain good hygiene. Likewise, if you're eating food that may be a little too hard for you to digest, since the mind and the body are quite sensitive from doing a lot of meditation, then eat easily digestible foods and drink plenty of hot liquids. Similarly, in the course of meditative practice if you start experiencing dread, anxiety, insomnia, or paranoia—be sensible. Maybe you are meditating in an imbalanced way; maybe you are dredging up something that is throwing you out of kilter. It might be a good idea to check it out with a trusted friend, or a clinical psychologist, or a savvy psychiatrist who has either meditated or who is familiar with meditation. Consult with a professional as you might check with a nutritionist about your food, should you be getting frequent stomachaches, or check with a medical internist if you are getting heartburn or headaches or what have you.

Having taken all sensible precautions, your nutritionist may tell you, "As far as I can tell, your diet is fine." The psychiatrist may say, "I don't see this as really being dangerous, it's just some of the stuff that comes up." The medical doctor says, "You don't have any illness that I can pinpoint." In which case, let it go and just say, "This is nyam." Then carry on in your practice. I think that's the balanced approach. The Teacher is warning us that when these types of nyam appear, we can become fixated exclusively on external causes—external demons, external illness, external stars. We can completely lose track of our practice, of the fundamental issue that this is all arising as a manifestation of our own mind. If we release it, the mind has an extraordinary capacity to heal itself. That's exactly what needs to happen—continue without grasping and let the mind settle.

> "When meditation is introduced with special terminology such as insight and so forth, there are many explanations of the stages of the path. Here, on our own path, mindfulness is presented as being like a cowherd, with thoughts like cows. Their steady, vivid manifestation, without interruption by various expressions of hope, fear, joy, and sorrow, is called enmeshed mindfulness.

"Insight," or *vipashyana*, as alluded to earlier, is a Buddhist technical term. "Enmeshed mindfulness" means that you still have mental phenomena to engage with. Like a fireworks display, they appear luminously, clearly, vividly. In the gaps between them you are not to inject expressions of grasping such as hope, fear, joy, and sorrow. These emotional vacillations can very easily arise in response to nyam. You may have an excellent session and think, "I'm really good at this. I think I can achieve shamatha." If your next session goes poorly, you think, "I doubt anyone has ever achieved shamatha. They're fooling us—it's just a myth." When such emotions arise, enticing you like Sirens, just be like space. The practice is really deliciously simple: "Settle your mind without distraction and without grasping." So enmeshed mindfulness means there are still phenomena arising in the mind. It doesn't mean you are grasping or becoming entangled with them.

It's vitally important to distinguish between this shamatha practice and "choiceless awareness," which has recently been introduced by popularizers of vipassana meditation. This shamatha practice entails focusing single-pointedly on thoughts and other mental events while ignoring, to the best of your ability, appearances to the five physical senses. When you cannot detect any thoughts occurring, then you focus on the space of the mind, still turning your attention away from the physical senses. As for choiceless awareness, there are no references to this term in any of the teachings of the Buddha recorded in the Pali language or in their authoritative commentaries, so it is misleading to present this as a vipassana practice. In reality, *choiceless awareness* is a term coined and defined by Jiddu Krishnamurti (1895–1986), who characterized it as the observation of whatever is occurring in the present moment, without any reaction, resistance, justification, or condemnation.[23] As helpful as this practice has proven to be, as it's been studied within the context of Mindfulness-Based Stress Reduction, it is neither a shamatha nor a vipashyana practice in any Buddhist tradition.

Such choiceless awareness also bears a strong similarity to "open presence," which a number of popularizers of Dzogchen teach these days. This practice consists simply of letting your awareness be open to all kinds of appearances, sensory and mental, while letting them come and go without intervention. "Open presence" is a very loose translation of the Tibetan term *rigpa chog zhag*, which literally means "resting in pristine awareness." This refers to the "breakthrough" phase of Dzogchen practice, and to engage in such authentic meditation, you must first gain an experiential realization of rigpa, and then simply rest—without distraction and without grasping—in this ultimate-ground state of consciousness. This practice is simply sustaining the Dzogchen view: viewing all phenomena from the perspective of rigpa. However, without having such realization of rigpa, one is simply resting in one's ordinary dualistic mind, like a marmot sunning on a rock, and this does not qualify as shamatha, vipashyana, or Dzogchen. Düdjom Lingpa ridicules such practice by citing the Tibetan aphorism, "The marmot ostensibly cultivating meditative stabilization is actually hibernating."[24]

In the Pali canon the Buddha does refer to a timeless, "nonmanifesting" dimension of consciousness that an arhat normally experiences only after death, when the continuum of one's conditioned consciousness ceases: "Where consciousness is signless, boundless, all-luminous, that's where earth, water, fire, and air find no footing... There 'name and form' are wholly destroyed."[25] Such nonmanifesting consciousness (that is, invisible to the ordinary, dualistic mind) appears to have the same characteristics of rigpa as it is presented in the Dzogchen tradition. According to the Buddhist sutras, one must be well versed in the practices of shamatha and vipashyana in order to gain such realization of unborn consciousness, and the same is true according to classic Dzogchen teachings. Padmasambhava declares: "Without genuine shamatha arising in one's mindstream, even if pristine awareness is pointed out, it may become nothing more than an object of intellectual understanding; one may be left simply giving lip service to the view, and there is the danger that one may succumb to dogmatism. Thus the root of all meditative states depends upon this, so do not be introduced to pristine awareness too soon, but practice until there occurs a fine experience of stability."[26]

SIGNS OF PROGRESS

"In general, these are some of the signs of progress for individuals who take appearances and awareness as the path:

At this point we get an extensive list of nyam that can occur as we progress. You meditate for a while and it's quite natural to want to know: "How am I doing? How far have I progressed? What are some signs of progress, or am I just treading water here? Am I doing something wrong?" Now keep in mind that the instructions are so simple that you should on the whole be able to figure out for yourself whether you're doing something wrong. They all boil down to the familiar phrase "Settle your mind without distraction, without grasping." If you are doing that while focusing single-pointedly on the space of the mind and its contents, that's pretty much it. If you're letting yourself be carried away, that implies distraction, so do your best to maintain unwavering mindfulness.

On the other hand, there may be times when you are not carried away, not distracted, but you still could be grasping. Something fascinating may arise, perhaps some very interesting, vivid images. "What's going to happen with that?" you wonder. As soon as the preference is there, as soon as you latch on to it, and moreover, especially if you are attending to the referent of the image, not just the image as an image, that's when grasping becomes locked in. For example, when a mental image of delicious food arises, if you get carried away, thinking about enjoying such a treat, you've been caught up in distraction and grasping. If you focus on the mental image of the food, and you are holding on to it because you're attracted to it, that's grasping. If you are simply mindful of that image, without being drawn to it and without wanting it to go away, you are practicing correctly. When you feel attracted to a thought or image or even an emotion, you might tell yourself, "I'm not distracted; I'm right here, right in the moment. I really like this." That too is grasping. So just be present, letting your awareness remain as still and as accommodating as space. It is very important to know clearly from moment to moment if you are practicing correctly or incorrectly.

In practices that are based on the development model, we are moving step by step to some designated goal, so we automatically have a means of gauging our progress. With this practice, however, it is so simple that you might easily wonder if any progress at all is being made. So here is the first sign of progress:

- the impression that all your thoughts are wreaking havoc in your body, speech, and mind, like boulders rolling down a steep mountain, crushing and destroying everything in their path

If that is coming up for you, you're really on the right path. Be aware, though, that the list of nyam presented here is only a short, generic one. Not having had this experience doesn't mean you should say, "Aw shucks! I'm off the track." This sign is just one of innumerable potential signs of progress. If you do have the sense that thoughts are crushing and destroying everything in the path of your body, speech, and mind, what should be your response? Simply continue practicing. Watch the boulders crashing. If you're not grasping on to them, you recognize that they're just images, just appearances.

Here are the other signs of progress listed in our text:

- a sharp pain in your heart as a result of all your thoughts, as if you had been pierced with the tip of a weapon

- the ecstatic, blissful sense that mental stillness is pleasurable but movement is painful

This may trigger a temptation to grasp on to stillness and ward off any kind of movement of the mind. Don't prefer stillness over movement. Whatever arises, let it be, without grasping on to either.

- the perception of all phenomena as brilliantly colored particles
- intolerable pain throughout your body, from the tips of the hair on your head down to the tips of your toenails

If this pain is a nyam and not a medical condition, your doctor will tell you, "This is a psychosomatic condition, there's nothing wrong with you that I can see."

- the sense that even food and drink are harmful, as a result of being tormented by a variety of the four hundred and four types of identifiable, complex disorders of wind, bile, phlegm, and so on

This is a reference to a standard classification of illnesses in Tibetan medicine. You may feel that you don't even want to eat or drink because you just feel uneasy about taking anything into your body. You are afraid doing so will make you nauseated.

- an inexplicable sense of paranoia about meeting other people, visiting their homes, or being in town

This is one of those pointless dreads. You are meditating, the mind becomes still, and then an intense rush of fear comes over you. It has no real focus. You really can't pinpoint what you are afraid of. Gen Lamrimpa commented during the one-year shamatha retreat he led in 1988: "When that happens, do not grasp on to it. Stand back from it and simply look at it. And then you'll disempower it. But if you latch on to it, you'll make yourself very unhappy, and your condition will go from bad to worse."

- compulsive hope in medical treatment, divinations, and astrology

That is, things start going haywire in your body, triggering paranoia, and you think, "If I could only find a better doctor. I heard of one in Argentina. Maybe I should travel there." Or you look to divinations: "I've heard of one lama whose divinations are said to be very good. I'll bet he could tell me something that would get me out of this mess." Or: "I need a newer, more accurate astrological chart to figure this out."

- such unbearable misery that you think your heart will burst

Sometimes waves of utter grief will just wash over you. You may or may not know what catalyzed it. Just watch it come, watch it go. See if you can observe misery from the perspective of a non-miserable awareness. That's really useful, especially when it's not clearly catalyzed by an external event. Let it simply unravel and disappear right back into the space of the mind.

- insomnia at night, or fitful sleep like that of someone who is critically ill

Indeed, all kinds of bizarre things can happen at night.

- grief and disorientation when you wake up, like a camel that has lost its beloved calf

You may experience merely a little passing disorientation, but it could also be pretty strong. The grief of a mother camel that has lost her young is a legendary example.

- the conviction that there is still some decisive understanding or knowledge you must have, and yearning for it like a thirsty person longing for water

What you are getting from the practices of the *Vajra Essence* somehow seems inadequate. You think in desperation, "There must be some lama out there who can give me a special oral transmission that would solve everything."

- **the emergence, one after another, of all kinds of thoughts stemming from the mental afflictions of the five poisons, so that you must pursue them, as painful as this may be**

The five poisons are delusion, craving, hostility, envy, and pride. What's described here can be likened to experiences of the after-death bardo. You sit down quietly, unafflicted, and out of the blue afflictions start bubbling up. They are like a vortex, grabbing you and then sucking you in. If you can practice with this and not be carried away, that's a very good preparation for the bardo.

- **various speech impediments and respiratory ailments**

"All kinds of experiences can occur—called experiences because all thoughts are expressions of the mind, where all appearances of joys and sorrows are experienced as such and cannot be articulated—yet all experiences of joys and sorrows are simultaneously forgotten and vanish.

There is just so wide a range—an infinite array of them. All of this stuff arises due to the lead weight of your awareness sinking down through the sedimentary layers of your psyche and stirring these things up. Don't grasp on to them, including the grief and the misery and the insomnia and so forth. Don't grasp on to them; just relax and be present with them, without grasping and without dissociation. Each one of them, both the joys and the sorrows, the positive and the negative, can wrap you into knots. "I really want that. I hope this happens. I hope that doesn't happen. I wish this would stop! I hope this never stops!" Whenever this happens, your mind becomes distorted (*klishta*). *Klesha*, a Sanskrit word, means a mental affliction, and *klishta* is a cognate of the same word. *Klishta* means "twisted." When the mind is afflicted, it's twisted. All these perturbations, all these vacillations, all these imbalances of the emotions, each one is warping the space of your mind. It's tightening you up around joys and hopes, around sorrows and fears. In each case, if you could just breathe out and relax and untwist, it would resolve itself.

So this is a practice of deepening relaxation such that stability simply emerges out of deepening levels of relaxation. As the stability deepens because the relaxation is deepening, then clarity and vividness arise right out of the stability. Relaxing then goes deeper, and as you become more and more relaxed, like cream coming from milk, the stability of the mind just naturally emerges from relaxation. Then, in turn, as the relaxation goes deeper, the stability goes deeper. As stability goes deeper, then further clarity emerges out of the stability. Likening the growth of shamatha to the growth of a tree, the deeper the roots of relaxation extend, the stronger the trunk of stability; and the stronger the stability, the higher grow the branches and foliage of vividness. All three qualities of relaxation, stability, and vividness emerge synergistically, just as the roots, trunk, and branches grow together, nourishing each other.

Images start to arise that are three-dimensional and luminously clear, and you didn't do anything to make that happen; it happens spontaneously. Two types of vividness emerge through this process. One we can call temporal vividness, by which you are able to detect increasingly brief mental events—thoughts, images, impulses—that previously went by so quickly you never noticed them. The other is qualitative vividness. This enables you to detect increasingly subtle mental processes that may linger for seconds on end, but so quietly and unobtrusively that they escaped your attention until now. With such enhanced vividness of both kinds, mental states and processes that were previously unconscious are now illuminated with the clear light of consciousness. This truly becomes a path of knowing yourself in the sense of plumbing the depths of your own mind.

Having said that, in this practice, like in any other shamatha practice, there is a balance of neither falling into laxity nor being caught up in excitation. There is a balance between the two all the way down to the subtlest levels of excitation and laxity. It's a question of balance. Here are some more possibilities for nyam:

- the conviction that there is some special meaning in every external sound you hear and form you see; thinking, 'That must be a
  sign or omen for me'; and compulsively speculating about the
  chirping of birds and everything else you see and feel

That can easily come up—yet one more Siren to seduce you.

- the sensation of external sounds and voices of humans, dogs,
  birds, and so on, all piercing your heart like thorns

The mind can and will become extremely sensitized in this process. When
you are sitting quietly and begin hearing sounds, even subtle sounds, they
can be piercing.

- unbearable anger due to having paranoid thoughts that everyone
  is gossiping about you and disparaging you

You may find this ridiculous anger welling up. If you have some proclivity
toward this brand of paranoia, as you plumb your depths it will appear and
it will seem to be very real. This provides you the opportunity to look at it
closely and then release it. This is really deep therapy.

- negative reactions when you hear and see others joking around
  and laughing, thinking that they are making fun of you, and retal-
  iating verbally
- compulsive longing for others' happiness when you watch them,
  due to your own experience of suffering

You may think of those good old days before you heard about Dharma and
how much fun you had. You think of all of those happy people who are just
enjoying life—enjoying movies, music, HDTV, good food, and sex, without a bit of guilt. How much fun they are having just killing time! You may
long for that and regret having connected with Dharma.

- fear and terror about weapons and even your own friends, because your mind is filled with a constant stream of anxieties
- everything around you leading to all kinds of hopes and fears

You are surrounded by Sirens tempting you in every manner. Everything is catalyzing hope and fear. You watch their arising and you let them go.

- premonitions of others who will come the next day, when you get into bed at night
- uncontrollable fear, anger, obsessive attachment, and hatred when images arise—seeing others' faces, forms, minds, and conversations, as well as demons and so forth, preventing you from falling asleep

As the mind becomes clearer or more transparent, luminous images will appear, arousing all manner of strong emotional responses. This is especially common when you are falling asleep and you pass into hypnogogic imagery (patterns and images that appear when you fall asleep consciously). They can be really wild and strong. Just release them.

- weeping out of reverence and devotion to your gurus, or out of your faith and devotion in the Three Jewels, your sense of renunciation and disillusionment with samsara, and your heartfelt compassion for sentient beings

It may well up out of the blue and rush through you, causing you to weep openly. Some may interpret this as a sign of difficulty in your meditation. Others may say it is a sign of your going very deep. Again, don't grasp on to it. Just let it pass on through. Be like a tourist traveling from the surface of your mind all the way down into its depths. Don't become a homesteader until you reach your destination—the substrate consciousness.

- the vanishing of all your suffering and the saturation of your mind with radiant clarity and ecstasy, like pristine space, although such radiant clarity may be preceded by rough experiences

There's no rule though that such experiences will necessarily be preceded by "rough experiences." It is different for everyone.

- the feeling that gods or demons are actually carrying away your head, limbs, and vital organs, leaving behind only a vapor trail, or merely having the sensation of this happening, or experiencing it in a dream

This is "involuntary chö"—the practice of offering your body as food for demons—somehow occurring spontaneously. This may appear to be occurring in a dream. Even so, it may be very realistic. You may have the sense that they are merely dreamlike apparitions, but you may also have a sense of complete dismemberment. That's a good sign, a sign of progress that you are really far along.

"Afterward, all your anguish vanishes, and you experience a sense of ecstasy as if the sky had become free of clouds. In the midst of this, the four kinds of mindfulness and various pleasant and harsh sensations may occur.

The four kinds of mindfulness are the four applications of mindfulness— mindfulness of body, feelings, mental states, and mental objects. Normally you practice this matrix of vipashyana techniques sequentially. But here, in the course of just doing this practice, the insights of these four applications or foundations of mindfulness may arise spontaneously. So this practice— which is ostensibly a practice of shamatha, designed to bring you to the substrate consciousness as a foundation for realizing emptiness and rigpa— may, as an unexpected dividend give you some very profound insights into impermanence, suffering, and no-self, which are characteristic of vipashyana practice.

"Spiritual friends who teach this path properly must know and realize that these experiences are not the same for everyone, so bear this in mind!

So far we have been given a short list of appearances that may arise as we deepen our shamatha practice. You may experience just a few of those he's described. Below, the Teacher is going to provide more detail, including the kind of experiences typical of people with certain psychophysical constitutions. Although some of these appearances are quite appalling, what's encouraging is that none of this is being introduced from some outside source. These experiences are not being inserted into our minds by the buddhas, teachers, or anyone else. These afflictions are there, in our minds, to begin with. They are the product of our beginningless cycling in samsara. We are fortunate now in being able to deal with them under laboratory conditions. In conducive circumstances this practice allows us to catalyze that which lies between our ordinary conscious awareness and the substrate consciousness. In contrast, most people are passing through these kinds of experiences in the course of ordinary life blindly—one life after another. As such, they are continually doing the "natural thing": they grasp on to everything that comes up; and by so doing they perpetuate samsara.

NYAM EMANATING FROM DIFFERENT PSYCHOPHYSICAL CONSTITUTIONS

> "For a person with a fire constitution, a sense of joy is prominent; for one with an earth constitution, a sense of dullness is prominent; for one with a water constitution, a sense of clarity is prominent; for one with an air constitution, harsh sensations are prominent; and for one with a space constitution, a sense of vacuity is prominent.

Of course we all have each of the five elements (the four elements mentioned earlier, plus space) as part of our psychophysical constitution, but what are the types of nyam likely to arise for each element specifically, for the element that predominates in a given person? If you are someone for whom the fire element is strongest, as you are coursing through shamatha, a sense of joy may be prominent. With the earth constitution, "a sense of dullness is prominent." That means you have to deal with and counteract laxity. For those with a water constitution, "a sense of clarity is prominent," which implies that you may become hypersensitive. For those with an air constitution, "harsh sensations are prominent"—not only physical aches and pains, but also mental harshness as well as anger and hatred. "And for one with a space constitution, a sense of vacuity," that is, being "spaced out," is dominant. Whichever cards you are dealt due to your constitutional inheritance, deal with it. That's just your karma. Besides even harsh sensations are not necessarily worse than having bliss or joy, because those can be a lot more seductive than a harsh sensation. So, don't be too quick to envy someone else with another type of constitution.

Now we are given the essential view:

ACCOMPLISHING THE PRACTICE

> "After all pleasant and harsh sensations have disappeared into the space of awareness—by just letting thoughts be, without having to do anything with them—all appearances lose their capacity to help or harm, and you can remain in this state.

The space of awareness is none other than the substrate. The Sanskrit term is *dhatu*, "space." The space of awareness, *within the context of the ordinary mind*, is just the ground-space of the ordinary mind, the substrate. Having not grasped on to all these pleasant and harsh sensations—and thereby not revitalized them, not giving them more juice and more power—you've just let them arise, untangle, and dissolve of their own accord, and then they have disappeared back into the space of the mind. So whatever the particular appearances are, they are relegated to being "just appearances." They have lost their power and you have gained control. You have regained your own birthright, so to speak—like an absent king who has finally returned and regained his own territory, which was originally lost and carried away by all this grasping.

Generally in Buddhism, self-grasping is associated with our relationship to the *skandhas*, the five psychophysical aggregates comprised of the body, feelings, recognition, compositional factors, and the six kinds of consciousness (mental consciousness and the five sensory modes of consciousness). As long as self-grasping is dominating your life, those five psychophysical aggregates are said to be "closely held." Why? Because when we observe the bodies of ourselves and others, we think, "My body. Not my body. My body..." Feelings give rise to "my feelings," and so on down the line. They are nothing more than phenomena arising in the space of your mind. Because they are closely held, though—"my feelings, my recognition, my thoughts"—an abundance of mental factors and processes arise. Then consciousness itself arises—"my consciousness." Because these aggregates are closely held, they can and do brutalize us.

Our text is directing us to the core aggregate—the mind. We are learning how to be vividly *aware of it* instead of holding it closely. There is no withdrawal and we respond with no repression or denial. Rather, we are luminously aware of whatever comes up—we are not grasping. Therefore these processes lose their ability to harm us. We can remain in that state by achieving shamatha. We achieve equipoise. This is sanity; we are emotionally balanced, attentionally balanced, and cognitively balanced. We now have a mind that is serviceable and ready to do whatever we wish. Moreover, since our afflictions are attenuated, this is no longer fertile ground for the afflictions to continue to arise. One of the little dividends is bliss. We experience a sense of bliss or joy that is quiet and serene—the joy of shamatha.

When you actually achieve shamatha, you receive a radical refinement or "tune-up" of all your vital energies. Regard this as a kind of "extreme makeover" of the body and mind, if you like. At that time there is a temporary, transient phase of ecstasy, during which you can do little beyond simply going with the flow. Then it tapers off, it becomes subdued, and what lingers—like background radiation of the "big bang of shamatha"—is a quiet, percolating, radiating sense of serenity, joy that is very malleable. It is malleable in the sense that you are not so overwhelmed with bliss that you cannot feel compassion and loving-kindness. This becomes your ground state, your new base camp for ascending to the heights of authentic vipashyana and Dzogchen practice.

"You may also have an extraordinary sense of bliss, luminosity, and nonconceptuality, visions of gods and demons, and a small degree of

extrasensory perception. The channels and elements function differently from one person to the next, so those with dominant earth
and air elements do not commonly experience extrasensory perception or visionary experiences. Extrasensory perception and
visions are chiefly experienced by people with a prominent fire or
water element.

These perceptions come straight out as a dividend of shamatha. They are
extraordinary—out of the ordinary—since they are not stimulus driven.
They result from the mental balance you have achieved. The fact that
extrasensory perception and visionary experiences are usually perceived by
those of the fire and water element constitution does not mean that if you
are earth, air, or space dominant you cannot develop extrasensory perception. For some people dominated by the other psychophysical constituents,
it will just flow right out of their practice, but for earth, air, and space
people, even after having achieved shamatha, they will still need to do a little extra to develop those abilities.[27]

When I was engaging in a six-month solitary retreat focusing on this
practice from the *Vajra Essence*, I occasionally drove ten miles to the nearest
pay phone to call my teacher, Gyatrul Rinpoche, when questions arose. He
made a couple of comments that may be pertinent to you at some point.
One of them was, "Alan, when you're meditating, you're doing so with too
much desire. When you're practicing, don't desire anything at all. Just do
the practice—with no hopes and fears." To that I replied, "Well, Rinpoche,
the whole issue of renunciation and bodhichitta is to develop this strong
yearning, this deep yearning to achieve enlightenment, and shamatha is
one of the critical ingredients. I've been practicing Dharma now for more
than twenty-five years, developing such a yearning, this aspiration, and
now you tell me to forget it? And then all the prayers of supplication—
'Bless me that I may realize . . .'—that's all an expression of desire. So, if I am
to practice without desire, what is the point of all these aspirations, including bodhichitta itself?"

Rinpoche replied, "Between sessions, bring to mind all the aspirations
and prayers you like. But when you are practicing, just do the practice."

Another point was, "Alan, make sure you also practice when you're lying down." That is wonderful advice, for the body can become very sore by sitting in meditation for many hours each day.

A third comment he made was quintessential: "Alan, when you're doing this practice right, without grasping, even if a thousand maras rose up to attack you, whatever your maras are, they could not inflict any injury if you're not grasping. And even if a thousand buddhas appeared to you, they couldn't do you any good. They don't need to. You don't need anything from those thousands of images of buddhas. Just continue practicing." So, whatever comes up, simply continue practicing as you were.

6

ACCOMPLISHING SHAMATHA

"Now, to classify the different levels by name, superior vision with single-pointed mindfulness, in which movement and mindfulness are united, is called 'insight.' If a sense of stillness predominates at this time, it is called the 'union of quiescence and insight.' In what way is this vision superior? Previously, even if you watched with great diligence, your mind was veiled by subconscious movement and by laxity and dullness, so thoughts were hard to see. But now, even without exerting yourself very much, all thoughts that arise become apparent, and you detect them very well.

The different levels he will name are stages through which you will pass. The first is *insight*. Here, "insight" is not to be confused with vipashyana, and it doesn't necessarily mean insight into the nature of emptiness or rigpa. It simply means exceptional insight into some facet of reality. In this case, it is the fusion of motion and stillness. Here the space of your awareness is still. Why? Because you are not grasping. You can sense your attention being in motion when you are grasping on to objects, pulling you this way and that, with either craving or aversion. In this case, insofar as you release the grasping, your awareness will remain still, even in the midst of, or simultaneously with, the movements of your mind. This is called the "fusion of stillness and motion," when your awareness remains still even while your thoughts are in motion.

In the midst of that insight, "if a sense of stillness predominates at this time, it is called the 'union of quiescence and insight.'" There is an absence of excitation. "In what way is this vision superior? Previously," before getting to this stage of the practice, "even if you watched with great diligence, your mind was veiled by subconscious movement and by laxity and dullness, so thoughts were hard to see." Right now your mind is veiled by subtle "murmurings" and, of course, by laxity and dullness. These subtle perturbations don't permit you enough clarity to see what's going on, and so some thoughts are difficult to see, such as these underlying murmurings. Once you do see them, you might say, "Oh, that was coming from the subconscious." Well, they were in the "subconscious" before, simply because you weren't conscious of them. Improve your clarity and the subconscious starts to come into view. Continue honing your attention until you probe all the way through the subconscious to the substrate consciousness, from which even subconscious mental events emerge.

So you arrive at the unification of movement and mindfulness. "But now, even without exerting yourself very much, all thoughts that arise become apparent, and you detect them very well." This is reminiscent of the Buddha's assertion, "For one who clings, motion exists; but for one who clings not, there is no motion. Where no motion is, there is stillness. Where stillness is, there is no craving. Where no craving is, there is neither coming nor going. Where no coming nor going is, there is neither arising nor passing away. Where neither arising nor passing away is, there is neither this world nor a world beyond, nor a state between. This, verily, is the end of suffering."[28] This practice of shamatha is a straight path to the liberation eventually realized through the union of shamatha and vipashyana.

> "As for the experiential visions at this stage, some yogins see everything, wherever they look, as forms of deities and as vibrant *bindus*. Some see different seed syllables, lights, and various other forms. Some perceive buddhafields; unfamiliar lands; melodies, songs, and speeches by various unknown beings; and a multitude of all sorts of viras and dakinis dancing and displaying various expressions. To some, all sights, sounds, smells, tastes, and tactile sensations appear

as signs and omens. Some have the sense of clairvoyantly observing many entities with and without form.

Again, these experiential visions indicate that the practice is simply percolating through and catalyzing the sedimentary layers of your psyche. By this stage you are pretty much finished with the experiences outlined in that somewhat horrific list given above. Instead you may have visions, which should not be mistaken for realizations, and "some yogins see everything, wherever they look, as forms of deities and as vibrant *bindus.*" That can happen spontaneously. You are not visualizing internally as you would in deity practice. Rather these *bindus* simply arise spontaneously in your visual field.

Furthermore, "some see different seed syllables, lights, and various other forms. Some perceive buddhafields; unfamiliar lands; melodies, songs, and speeches by various unknown beings; and multitudes of all sorts of viras and dakinis"—viras, recall, are heroic beings and enlightened bodhisattvas. Dakinis are essentially female bodhisattvas. These will most likely be appearing in the space of your mind.

"To some"—in this case when looking out in the world all around you, in between meditative sessions—"all sights, sounds, smells, tastes, and tactile sensation appear as signs and omens." The world appears to be pregnant with meaning. "Some have the sense of clairvoyantly observing many entities with and without form." These may be mere apparitions or, as he stated earlier, people with fire and water constitutions may very well gain some clairvoyance at this point in their practice.

How are we to look at the emergence of these mundane siddhis? Are these visions of viras and dakinis and buddhafields coming only from the ground-space of your own mind, the substrate? Is this space of the mind porous? Of course things such as karma can sink down into it from our personal experiences in this lifetime and from the past, but can influences and experiences from the primordial ground seep through it from below—from rigpa? Might something be flowing from the mind of your guru, who is blessing your mindstream, blessing you from a deeper stratum—not just catalyzing something in your own substrate consciousness? When we see viras and dakinis or buddhafields, perhaps they are emerging from the depths below. Then it is quite possible that we may be opening up a conduit of blessings, a conduit of imagery, of various things that are actually coming from something deeper than the substrate consciousness. This is, in fact, the case. The substrate consciousness has now become transparent, porous, so things flow through it more easily from below, from rigpa.

For example, it's clear that by achieving shamatha you arrive at the transparency of the ground of the ordinary mind such that, with a little effort and through skillful means, you can develop clairvoyance. Having achieved the transparency of this ground, you may experience remote viewing or clairaudience or knowledge of another person's mind in the present moment. This is not like a memory, something out of the past. Rather you are connected with something taking place now, spatially removed from your location, in someone else's mindstream. Clearly, abilities such as these yield experiences that are not limited to your substrate consciousness. So it appears that from the platform of shamatha—even though you have not yet mastered the ground awareness, or rigpa, buddha nature—you can get these "sneak previews." You are able to dip your cup into the ocean of rigpa and bring out a little thimbleful. That is what is meant by mundane siddhis. This may be a useful model for understanding some of these extraordinary experiences.

"After meditating deeply in this way, any sense of joy or sorrow may trigger a unification of mindfulness and conceptualization. Then, like the knots in a snake uncoiling, everything that appears dissolves into the external environment. Subsequently, everything appears to vanish by itself, resulting in a natural release. Appearances and awareness become simultaneous, so that events seem to be released as soon as they are witnessed. Thus, emergence and release are simultaneous. As soon as things emerge from their own space, they are released back into their own space, like lightning flashing from the sky and vanishing back into the sky. Since this appears by looking within, it is called *liberation in the expanse*. All these are in fact the unification of mindfulness and appearances, entailing single-pointed focus of attention.

Joy and sorrow normally arouse grasping. In this case however, instead of catalyzing grasping, they may trigger the unification of mindfulness and conceptualization. You are right there in that unity, dwelling in the still spaciousness of your awareness and seeing the movement of joys and sorrows arising. "Then, like the knots in a snake uncoiling, everything that appears dissolves into the external environment." Because there is so little grasping occurring even between sessions, when you see appearances arising you are completely present with them, and they dissolve right back into the space of the mind. Rather than chunky things moving around, banging into each other, you see appearances arise from space and then dissolve back into external space, until "everything appears to vanish by itself..." As you go deeper into the nature of awareness, into samadhi, your mind is drawn in as if you were falling asleep, yet it remains luminously aware. Thus everything appears to vanish by itself, just like the whole world vanishes for you when you fall asleep.

Here you draw your awareness in, and it results in a "natural release." Because there is no grasping, appearances and awareness are released as soon as they are observed. They are not crystallized into "things" due to grasping, "so that events seem to be released as soon as they are witnessed." They are just arising and vanishing. "Thus, emergence and release," arising and dissolution, "are simultaneous." Where normally you would grasp and reify, you are seeing only a flux. This doesn't indicate the realization of emptiness, but reification has become relatively dormant. "As soon as things emerge from their own space," whether it's external space or internal space, "they are released back into their own space, like lightning flashing from the sky and vanishing back into the sky." They are instantaneously gone.

"Since this appears by looking within, it is called *liberation in the expanse.*" Expanse, of course, is of your own awareness. This is why it is crucial in this practice to focus single-pointedly on the space of the mind and its contents and not be equally open to all other appearances from the senses. If you continue to be interested in sensory impressions, your mind will not withdraw into the substrate. Moreover, since in such open presence you are engaging with appearances of the desire realm, your awareness will not withdraw into the form realm, which is a defining characteristic of achieving shamatha, or access to the first dhyana.

"All these are in fact the unification of mindfulness and appearances, entailing single-pointed focus..." The author has used a number of different terms throughout: taking the mind as the path, taking appearances and awareness as the path, taking mindfulness of appearances as the path. These all refer to the same thing—the practice of settling the mind in its natural state. At this point they are all unified—arising and falling, arising and falling, moment by moment—with no grasping on to either subject or object.

> "After all pleasant and unpleasant experiential visions have dissolved into the space of awareness, consciousness rests in its own stainless, radiant clarity. Whatever thoughts and memories arise, do not cling to these experiences; do not modify or judge them, but let them arise as they rove to and fro. In doing so, the effort involved in vivid, steady apprehension—as in the case of thoughts apprehended by tight mindfulness—vanishes of its own accord. Such effort makes the dissatisfied mind compulsively strive after mental objects. Sometimes, feeling dissatisfied, as if you're lacking something, you may compulsively engage in a lot of mental activity entailing tight concentration and so on.

When the Teacher speaks of consciousness resting in its own "stainless, radiant clarity," this is not in reference to rigpa. In this context these phenomena are taking place within the domain of the mind. Here, "space of awareness" means the substrate. We must take care with the term "stainless." Within the Dzogchen context, the dharmakaya is stainless; emptiness is stainless; buddha nature is stainless. Once you have fully realized that ultimate ground, you are a buddha—job done! In this context, though, the text is referring to the substrate, which is stainless in the more limited sense that none of the coarse mental afflictions are presently manifesting; rather they are merely dormant. Even so, that's pretty marvelous. Having experienced many of the pleasant and unpleasant mental phenomena mentioned previously, you have essentially run the gamut of your mind—from the surface level of easily detectable mental processes all the way down to the substrate consciousness. Now these phenomena dissolve right back into the space of the mind and consciousness rests in its own stainless clarity— the very nature of consciousness itself.

"Whatever thoughts and memories arise, do not cling to these experiences; do not modify or judge them, but let them arise as they rove to and fro." Although you have not yet achieved shamatha, you are really well on the way. At times now you may have significant intervals where nothing manifests—no pleasant or unpleasant visions or emotions—allowing you to settle into serenity, into something very close to the substrate consciousness. Things do get very calm after about the sixth of the nine mental stages prior to shamatha.

"In doing so," in practicing correctly, "the effort involved in vivid, steady apprehension—as in the case of thoughts apprehended by tight mindfulness—vanishes of its own accord." Since you are pretty far along the path now, when you observe very carefully, that is, when you magnify your attention, the effort of that vivid, steady apprehension just evaporates.

In this practice the greatest effort comes at the beginning. In the final stages, it's just effortless. Having said that, please do not think that you have to give *maximum* effort at the beginning. That would be overdoing it. "Doing your best" is not "trying your hardest." Given the balance of relaxation, stability, and vividness required, trying your hardest is trying way too hard. So in the course of the practice of shamatha, whatever technique you are following, the degree of effort you need to exert to practice correctly tapers off as you approach accomplishment, and then simply vanishes. You will have far greater stability and vividness than you started off with, but the effort to maintain and establish that vivid, steady apprehension vanishes of its own accord. "Such effort"—trying too hard—"makes the dissatisfied mind compulsively strive after mental objects." You arrive at a point in the practice where, if you keep on exerting effort, keep on applying introspection to try to fix something, you're actually cluttering up your practice.

In many ways this path of shamatha seems like a microcosm of the path of Dzogchen, to enlightenment itself. The fact that you could so easily mistake shamatha for enlightenment or the highest stage of Dzogchen is understandable. In the final stages of Mahamudra or Dzogchen you need only relax. You are on a conveyor belt to enlightenment, just as in the advanced stages of shamatha you are on a conveyor belt to the substrate consciousness. Effort is no longer required to achieve this lesser, but still very significant, accomplishment.

7

PITFALLS

In the course of this practice you may at times wonder, "What's going on? I'm really not doing anything. I am doing the practice correctly, but I am just sitting here. Maybe I should quit and get a job, or cultivate loving-kindness, or write a book—that's what the world needs." Such thoughts can easily appear, because you truly are *doing* so little. As Gyatrul Rinpoche once commented: "The problem with you Western students is not that you don't have enough faith in Buddhism. You don't have enough faith in yourselves." The very fact that you are doing nothing so luminously and clearly is facilitating subconscious processes—a balancing, a healing, an illumination, an opening up, a purification. You just don't trust the enormous healing capacity of your own awareness.

This is where understanding buddha nature as reality rather than as mere potential is crucial. From the perspective of an unenlightened sentient being, one *has* a buddha nature in the sense that one has the potential to achieve buddhahood; and it needs to be cultivated, or developed, for one to become enlightened. But from the perspective of a Dzogchen adept, or vidyadhara, you *are* your buddha nature, and you simply need to stop identifying with your ordinary body, speech, and mind (together with all your mental afflictions and obscurations) and to begin recognizing who you already are in order to be enlightened. From a Dzogchen perspective the primary difference between unenlightened sentient beings and buddhas is that the former don't know who they are, and the latter do. The ancient maxim "Know thyself" now takes on infinite significance.

HAZARDS IN THE LATER STAGES OF SHAMATHA PRACTICE

"In this phase, consciousness comes to rest in its own state; mindfulness emerges, and because there is less clinging to experiences, consciousness settles into its own natural, unmodified state. In this way, you come to a state of naturally settled mindfulness. This experience is soothing and gentle, with clear, limpid consciousness that is neither benefited nor harmed by thoughts, and you experience a remarkable sense of stillness, without needing to modify, reject, or embrace anything.

Here Düdjom Lingpa is describing the final phases of shamatha. "In this way, you come to a state of naturally settled mindfulness." Recall how he described an earlier phase when an abundance of mental phenomena was arising. He warned that as you initiate this practice you shouldn't expect your thoughts to vanish. What you could hope for would be to maintain your presence with them, without distraction, without grasping. That was called *enmeshed mindfulness*—not because it's all confused or mixed together, but because you are engaged with the phenomena arising in your mind.

Further down the line you move into the interim stages already spoken of, where the occurrence of appearances and dissolution is simultaneous. Due to the power of mindfulness there is a unification of mindfulness and appearances. This occurs sometime during the middle phase of this practice. Later still, the practice becomes more spacious, and there are periods of sheer stainless, radiant clarity. As you progress down the home stretch, there is just naturally settled mindfulness. Without requiring any artifice on your part, mindfulness has settled in its own way, of its own accord. You have brought sanity to yourself, to your awareness, and to your mind. That means you come to wholeness, to coherence—you have arrived at *naturally settled mindfulness*. The anchor has struck bottom.

With an experience that is "soothing and gentle, with clear, limpid consciousness that is neither benefited nor harmed by thoughts," and that carries "a remarkable sense of stillness, without needing to modify, reject, or embrace anything," if you haven't achieved shamatha yet, you are really close.

> "If you are not counseled by a good spiritual friend at this time, you might think, 'Now an extraordinary, unparalleled view and meditative state have arisen in my mindstream; this is difficult to fathom and can be shared with no one.' After placing your trust and conviction in this without discussing it with anyone, you may delude yourself for a while. Even if you discuss your situation with a spiritual friend, unless that person knows how to listen critically and responds in a persuasive fashion, you will stray far from the path. If you get stuck here for the rest of your life, you will be tied down and prevented from transcending the realm of mundane existence. Therefore, be careful!

Now, a cautionary note: Having arrived at this point in your meditation, you may think, "I've hit the bonanza—this is dharmakaya! This is so transcendental and holy that I doubt that anyone's ever experienced it before. If I told anybody else about it, they would never be able to understand it. Therefore, I had better keep it to myself."

"After placing your trust and conviction in this, without discussing it with anyone, you may delude yourself for a while. Even if you discuss your situation with a spiritual friend, *unless that person knows how to listen critically...*" Having that ability means that your spiritual friend really understands the context, sees how you've gotten to where you are. Context is vitally important here because this description could relate to Dzogchen or to becoming a vidyadhara. A wise spiritual friend will see the context, will notice the subtlety in what is going on, and will be able to give you good advice. So, "unless that person knows how to listen critically and responds in a persuasive fashion, you will stray far from the path."

In reaching this level you have arrived at a remarkable place, but if you cling to it and believe this is ultimate, then you will stray far from the path. "If you get stuck here for the rest of your life, you will be tied down and prevented from transcending the realm of mundane existence. Therefore, be careful!" This caveat is echoed in the teachings of Tsongkhapa, Karma Chagmé Rinpoche, and many other great lamas. It must have happened many, many times for them to keep on repeating it and repeating it until everybody hears it: "You will very, very easily think you're enlightened." This is where the tradition, the lineage—having truly wise people to consult who are further along the path than us—is really important. So do be careful.

> "In particular, the experience of clarity may result in visions of gods and demons, and you may think that you are suddenly being assaulted by demons. At times this might even be true; however, by thinking you are clairvoyant and repeatedly fixating on gods and demons, eventually you will feel that you are being overcome by demons. In the end, by mentally conjuring up gods and demons and spreading the word that you are clairvoyant, your meditation will be all about demons, and your mind will be possessed by them. Then your vows and sacred commitments will deteriorate, you will stray far from Dharma, become lost in the mundane activities of this life, and befuddle yourself with magic rituals. As you pursue food and wealth—without even a trace of contentment—clinging, attachment, and craving will ensnare your mind. If you die in this state, you will be reborn as a malevolent demon. Having accumulated the causes of experiencing the environment and suffering of a sky-roving hungry ghost, your view and meditation will go awry, and you will remain deluded endlessly in samsara.

How is it that "the experience of clarity"—luminosity—"may result in visions of gods and demons"? Our eyes are designed to pick up a very narrow bandwidth in the overall spectrum of electromagnetic radiation. Within that we see the colors of the visual spectrum, but we cannot see infrared or ultraviolet. In a general sense, shamatha is designed to widen your bandwidth of mental perception. For one thing, when you achieve shamatha you can experientially access dimensions of existence that were previously hidden from view. You've tapped into your substrate consciousness, which is transparent, and you have access to the form realm, where you may witness some of its inhabitants. This kind of access may allow you to see different types of sentient beings, gods, and so forth. Because your mind is no longer locked into being purely human and the phenomena of the desire realm, you may become a visionary.

As long as your base of operations is the five physical senses and the ordinary mind, you are tied to a human psyche, limiting your perception to those things that we are all accustomed to. If you are a Tibetan you might see a ghost once in a while. As soon as you've tapped into shamatha, you've accessed something that is nonhuman. The substrate consciousness is not a human state of consciousness, nor does it belong exclusively to some other class of sentient being within samsara. It encompasses all of those. All the mind-states of different classes of sentient beings emerge from the substrate consciousness. This means that potentially, if you access that common ground—that "stem consciousness"—you could conceivably see sentient beings of all the six realms of existence. You may even tap into memories of yourself in different incarnations. So the doors of perception are opened, and you may start seeing some creatures that ordinary people, with their limited bandwidth of mental perception, cannot see.

Therefore, "the experience of clarity may result in visions of gods and demons, and you may think that you are suddenly being assaulted by demons. At times this might even be true." Just as viruses and bacteria and radiation do exist even though most people can't see them, there exist other entities not normally visible to people lacking high degrees of samadhi, and some of them may be malevolent. So it is time to learn to don some armor. That is why in generation-stage practice and in Vajrayana practice in general there are "wheels of protection," protective devices, mantras, and so on. In fact, whole sections of this text are designed to help you develop your own defense field against malevolent forces.

The demons that trouble you may be alien entities or they might even be human. While Gen Lamrimpa was in solitary retreat in the Himalayas, a woodcutter, for no apparent reason, came to hate him and verbally abused him, even though Gen Lamrimpa was doing no more than meditating quietly in his hut. Strangely, just before the woodcutter died, he confessed to

Gen Lamrimpa, asked for his forgiveness, and passed away. What brought them together in this strange relationship was karma. So whether it is from the traditional Asian view an actual demon or just a difficult person abusing or slandering you for no apparent reason, you are bound to wonder, "What is that all about?" Well, that's just part of the path; it happens. Whether it's a bad back or a sick stomach—or people coming out of the woodwork to attack you—that's karma.

"By thinking you are clairvoyant and repeatedly fixating on gods and demons, eventually you will feel you are being overcome by demons." Even when you are getting near to achieving shamatha, things of this kind can still arise. Recall William James's aphorism, "For the moment, what we attend to is reality." When you start seeing apparitions—whether they are coming from some external source or purely from your substrate—if you start fixating on them, grasping on to them, obsessing about them, then you feed them, and you will be overrun by them. So we are given the very familiar advice: "Don't obsess. Don't fixate. Don't grasp."

When you are getting close to the substrate, your imagination is extremely powerful. If you want to visualize something, you can visualize it almost as well as if you are seeing it. Your dreams become very vivid. So the imagery that comes up, gods and demons and so forth, may be just full-blown, three-dimensional, "Technicolor with Dolby Sound" concoctions of your own substrate. Does being "imaginary" mean that they cannot harm you? After all, they are just hallucinations. Believe me, if you grasp on to them, they can indeed harm you. Witness the terrible misery schizophrenics suffer. As you reach these levels of samadhi, with your imagination becoming very potent, you must treat it with great intelligence. If you don't, if you conjure up these gods and demons, if you allow yourself to be overrun, "then by mentally conjuring up gods and demons and spreading the word that you are clairvoyant...in the end, your meditation will be all about demons, and your mind will be possessed by them."

"Then your vows and sacred commitments will deteriorate, you will stray far from Dharma, become lost in the mundane activities of this life, and befuddle yourself with magic rituals." As we saw in an earlier description of a similar situation, once you are possessed by demons you may feel compelled to find some great sorcerer or magician to whom you can ask, "How do I get out of this?" You will be given mantras to recite and concoctions to drink and ceremonies to perform. In this way you slip into the realm of the occult. People spend a long time, sometimes their whole lives, there. It has very little, if anything, to do with enlightenment, but since it is paranormal, many people find it seductive. In so doing they are befuddled with magical rituals. Let's not—we have better things to do.

"As you pursue food and wealth," because you may consider yourself something of a sorcerer or shaman at this point, "without even a trace of contentment—clinging, attachment, and craving will ensnare your mind. If you die in this state, you will be reborn as a malevolent demon." After all, at this point that's all you really care about, that's what you're fixating upon. "Having accumulated the causes of experiencing the environment and the suffering of a sky-roving hungry ghost, your view and meditation will go awry, and you will remain deluded." I would call that a pretty strong warning— "Beware! Skull and crossbones!" Instead of embarking on the voyage to shamatha and to enlightenment, you are joining the pirates—magic and the occult. It can definitely happen, especially when you start developing samadhi. With that you can open up a whole realm of paranormal experience, the psychic, the occult, and so forth. It can be one enormous trap leading absolutely nowhere. So let's skip that and continue practicing as before, maintaining the core of our refuge—bodhichitta.

> **"When people of average or inferior faculties enter this path, the signs of the path will surely occur, but if they cling to anything, they will be trapped again by that clinging. Knowing that such experiences are highly misleading and unreliable, leave your awareness in its own state, with no clinging, hope, fear, rejection, or affirmation. By so doing, these experiences will be spontaneously released in their own nature, like mist disappearing into the sky. Know this to be true!**

When reading the texts of so many of the practices to which I've been introduced, sometimes I feel quite intimidated—I'm just not up to snuff. I'm not like those professional meditators, the "real practitioners." Therefore,

I find these words refreshing: "When people of average or inferior faculties enter the path, the signs of the path will surely occur..." This practice is not for those with superior faculties only. Düdjom Lingpa is not letting us off the hook. We cannot shy away with self-effacing phrases like, "Aw shucks, I'm just not up to it."

Nonetheless, although the signs of the path will appear for those with average or inferior facilities, "if they cling to anything, they will be trapped again by that clinging." Of course we are not so likely to cling to the most negative phenomena—insomnia, depression, paranoia, and so on. We are more likely to cling to bliss, luminosity, and nonconceptuality and to visions. Excited by these, the general tendency is to feel a compulsion to tell somebody about it. That's like a gourd that is filled with just a little bit of water—shake it and it makes a big noise. In contrast, shake a gourd completely filled with water—those with deep realization—and there is no noise at all. The truly realized tend to be reserved about revealing their inner experiences to others. Occasionally, happily, there are great, truly enlightened beings who divulge their experience openly. That is what Düdjom Lingpa has done for our benefit. He told us he was a fully matured vidyadhara. Milarepa and a few others have spoken with the same frankness, and we should find that inspiring.

"Knowing that such experiences are highly misleading and unreliable"—here he is referring to nyam—"leave your awareness in its own state..." The author has revealed all these pitfalls and then given us the simple antidote: With all of these nyam, these intoxicating, "really cool" things ranging from *bindus* to buddhafields—along with their horrific, negative counterparts—"leave your awareness in its own state, with no clinging, hope, fear, rejection, or affirmation." When the demons come, don't give them a target. Let your awareness be like space. "By so doing, these experiences will be spontaneously released in their own nature, like mist disappearing into the sky. Know this to be true!"

> "O Vajra of Mind, there's no telling what specific types of good and
> bad experiences might arise. All techniques, from the achievement
> of quiescence until conscious awareness manifests, simply lead to

experiences, so anything can happen. Therefore, understand that identifying all these as experiences is a crucial point and the quintessence of practical advice. Then realize this and bear it in mind!"

The Teacher, addressing Bodhisattva Great Boundless Emptiness, has returned to his initial comments on this topic as a way of rounding off this discussion. The variation among the psyches, substrate consciousnesses, and karma of individuals is immensely complex. It is impossible to tell someone exactly what is going to happen between the initiation of shamatha meditation and its achievement. "All techniques, from the achievement of quiescence (*shamatha*) until conscious awareness manifests (*rigpa*), simply lead to experiences (*nyam*), so anything can happen. Therefore, understand that identifying all these as experiences"—simply as nyam—"is a crucial point and the quintessence of practical advice."

Underline that! Identify all these experiences as "just nyam." They vacillate like the score of a basketball game, coming and going like sunshine and rain, like bronchitis, like back problems, like everything else. "It's just nyam"—stuff that comes up in the course of the path. All of those seductive siddhis and horrific experiences—just let them be. On the morning of his enlightenment, all the maras appeared to the Buddha, which can be understood as external manifestations of troubling nyam. According to the early accounts in the Pali canon of the Buddha's life, even after his enlightenment the maras would still visit him. Although some modern popularizers of Buddhism like to interpret these only metaphorically as expressions of one's own neuroses, the traditional Buddhist view is that they are actually sentient beings, which suggests to me that they are not coming merely from the substrate. Maras would appear to the Buddha, testing him, saying, "Hey Gautama! You're not really enlightened, you're just fooling yourself." They'd try to trip him up. He had only one response for them: "Mara, I see you." Then, according to some accounts, the mara would become disappointed and vanish.

This practice presents both enormous possibilities and pitfalls, and fortunately Düdjom Lingpa has laid them out transparently. When they actually occur they tend to be overwhelming. At least memorize what to do when that happens. Understand that these are just nyam. "Then realize this and bear it in mind!" In other words, remember that when you are *actually practicing*. This is where the cultivation of mindfulness entails much more than merely being present with whatever appearances are arising here and now. In Buddhist practice mindfulness also means remembering the teachings you've received so that you can apply them when the appropriate situation arises. On merely hearing about depression, or a blank, nameless dread, or apparitions coming up, or nightmares or insomnias, or crushing boulders, or terrible pain throughout your body, we might smile and say, "Gee, that sounds pretty awful." When it starts happening to us, however, we may easily grasp at and reify it—not because we want to but because it seems overwhelming. The same goes for the more pleasant kinds of nyam. And yet the practice is very simple.

Nyam can also make assessing our progress tricky. Suppose that you are consistently practicing three hours a day within a relatively serene lifestyle and the practice seems to be moving along well. Then, suddenly, you feel you have regressed to the point where you were six months previously. You may ask yourself, "Have I made some mistake?" That is a possibility, and you may check your text, your notes, to see if you have erred—whether you have remembered to practice in accordance with authentic instructions. You could also speak with your teacher or with a Dharma companion. Ask, "Did I slip into some grasping? Did I fall into laxity or excitation and then not even recognize it?" Making such inquiries is what makes a good Dharma student.

If, on checking that, you conclude that you haven't made such an error, it may be that you have encountered yet another level of sedimentation of your psyche. The lead weight of your focused attention has brought you into contact with deeper strata of your mind and their associated nyam. There are some strata that are very clear, and the weight drops right through—you seem to have hit bottom—but you may now be at the beginning of another layer. It's not the same layer where you were earlier. It may look that way, but it's not. Now you get to deal with a new one. You will then move through the nyam, the meditative experiences of this new stratum. Even the clear, serene strata are also nyam. Don't confuse them with realization.

From the time you begin practicing "until conscious awareness mani-fests…"—though there are different ways of reading that, here "conscious awareness" refers to rigpa. So he is saying, "from now until your realization of rigpa, everything is nyam." From the ordinary, or relative, point of view, we must practice in order to purify our minds of our personal, karmic influ-ences, which often find expression as nyam. That is one legitimate per-spective, but we can also view this from the perspective of *pure vision*. Take the woodcutter who so harassed Gen Lamrimpa. We could say that situa-tion derived from karma, but to paraphrase Shantideva, if you have nobody to badger you, how will you accomplish the perfection of patience? Like-wise, if you have no one to whom you can give, no one who is in any need of something you have to offer, how are you going to develop the perfec-tion of generosity? You need to develop the six perfections. So you could say that in that particular phase of his practice, Gen Lamrimpa desperately needed somebody to be angry with him. He hadn't angered anyone, but the woodcutter appeared, nonetheless, as needed. From this perspective the woodcutter came as a pure blessing of the Buddha so that Gen Lamrimpa could grapple with anger and resentment and then develop deeper patience, forbearance, equanimity, and compassion. Therefore, along with all the material emanating from your mind with which you must grapple, situations may appear from outside that will enhance your practice.

From the perspective of pure vision, dealing with all of these thorny internal and external challenges will give you confidence born of maturity, wisdom, and virtue. You will become less prone to grasping and instability and will be able to handle your new capabilities, such as the siddhis men-tioned above, without getting thrown for a loop. Achieving that requires that you learn in stages, traversing the mind level by level, and deal with the external situations that must arise—all of which can be considered blessings from the Buddha.

So, with every arising challenge, if it's insomnia, great! Let your aware-ness become larger than the mental space occupied by insomnia. If it's para-noia, let your awareness be larger than the paranoia. If it's bodily pain, make your awareness bigger than that. Each time you do that you will discover that you are not just surmounting an obstacle, but that a transformation is taking place that was necessary for you to go further in your practice. This is why I have such confidence in shamatha. If in this practice you are going to acquire paranormal abilities, it is better for everyone that you are balanced and mature. Indeed, as we shall see directly, such transformations are the doorway to deeper practice.

THE ROLE AND SIGNIFICANCE OF SHAMATHA

> Then Great Boundless Emptiness asked, "O Bhagavan, if all experiences, whether pleasant or rough, are far from being the path to omniscience and bring no such benefit, why should we practice meditation? Teacher, please explain!"

If these meditative experiences resulting from shamatha practice are not rigpa—they do not have the benefit of enlightenment—why practice shamatha at all? Couldn't we just skip shamatha and go straight for Dzogchen, go directly to the ultimate?

> The Bhagavan replied, "O Vajra of Mind, when individuals with coarse, dysfunctional minds agitated by discursive thoughts enter this path, by reducing the power of their compulsive thinking, their minds become increasingly steady, and they achieve unwavering stability. On the other hand, even if people identify conscious awareness but do not continue practicing, they will succumb to the faults of spiritual sloth and distraction. Then, even if they do practice, due to absentmindedness they will become lost in endless delusion.

We enter shamatha practice with a dysfunctional mind, and leave with a functional mind—enter with disequilibrium, exit with equilibrium. That's the significance of this practice. Attaining a high degree of sanity might be a really good idea on the way to omniscience.

"On the other hand, even if people identify conscious awareness"— rigpa—even if they go to some sublime lama and get pointing-out instructions and get some authentic glimpse of rigpa, or if some insight, some taste of rigpa, comes to them out of the blue—"but do not continue practicing, they will succumb to the faults of spiritual sloth and distraction." So even if you get some taste of rigpa, unless you are able to take the ground as your path and sustain it, then it is very easy to lose it. You soon "succumb to the faults of spiritual sloth and distraction." Incidentally, I think our civilization gives us the greatest bounty of distractions of any civilization in human history.

Spiritual sloth is an easily misunderstood term. The medieval contemplative tradition of Christianity has a corresponding concept, which in Latin is called *acedia*, also often translated as "spiritual sloth." I believe this concept comes closest to the meaning of the Buddhist term. From the Tibetan, however, it is often translated as "laziness." Indeed, spiritual sloth may manifest as being a "couch potato." You could call that laziness, where you are really lethargic, sluggish—the heavy feeling of the earth element. But not all spiritual sloth expresses itself as laziness. Spiritual sloth manifests for fire and air people when they get caught up in one project after another—where they always have something going on, continually ensnared by one mundane activity after another. Each time they get caught up in such busyness, they always have the snappy reply, "Oh, but this is really important, because this is for the sake of sentient beings, and it's virtuous."

So spiritual sloth may manifest in a lazy, sluggish mode, or as hyperactivity—popping around doing good—which dissipates your energy. You amass merit—good karma—but you wind up spinning around in samsara. In other words, you can have some very deep meditative experience in Zen, in Dzogchen, Mahamudra, or in Vedanta, but you are left with nothing more than a memory. Then you spend the rest of your life going from one project to the next, always caught up in the little affairs of daily life, conscientiously meeting your deadlines, until finally the deadline you meet is your own death.

"Then, even if they do practice, due to absentmindedness they will become lost in endless delusion." By practicing Dzogchen without having a strong foundation in the practice of shamatha you can have a taste of rigpa. For continuity and real growth, however, you need a vessel that doesn't turn upside down so easily from distractions and emotional imbalances. If the mind is dysfunctional and you experience a little drop of rigpa, after years have passed it may remain as nothing more than a memory: "Gosh, that reminds me—you should have been there twenty-seven years ago. I had this really great experience!" You become lost in endless delusion.

EXPERIENCING THE SUBSTRATE CONSCIOUSNESS

"The mind, which is like a cripple, and vital energy, which is like a blind, wild stallion, are subdued by fastening them with the rope of meditative experience and firmly maintained attention. Once people of dull faculties have recognized the mind, they control it with the reins of mindfulness and introspection. Consequently, as a result of their experience and meditation, they have the sense that all subtle and coarse thoughts have vanished. Finally, they experience a state of unstructured consciousness devoid of anything on which to meditate. Then, when their awareness reaches the state of great non-meditation, their guru points this out, so that they do not go astray.

The dysfunctional mind, and vital energy—which is "like a blind, wild stallion"—are subdued, not hobbled, with the rope of the meditative experiences of bliss, luminosity, and nonconceptuality, and with continuous, focused attention. Continuity does not mean bursts of frenzy, of zeal, or applying ourselves to meditation intensely for short intervals and then slacking off. Continuity is "firmly maintained attention."

"Once people of dull faculties have recognized the mind, they control it with the reins of mindfulness and introspection." This is taking the mind as the path. "Consequently, as a result of their experiences"—nyam—"and meditation, they have the sense that all subtle and coarse thoughts have vanished." Over time, and at its own pace, the density of obsessive thoughts diminishes. They become progressively subtler as you simply let them be, let them dissolve, without compulsively being caught up and carried away by them. Eventually you attain equilibrium, an equipoise wherein coarse and even subtle thoughts have vanished. "Finally, they experience a state of unstructured consciousness," where there's nothing contrived.

Again, we're not talking about rigpa. We're talking about the substrate consciousness—unfabricated, unstructured, pre-human, more basic than human, more basic than any other life form—out of which all kinds of mundane mental states and processes emerge. In this way the substrate consciousness can be regarded as a "stem consciousness," analogous to a stem cell that can morph into a wide variety of highly specified cells depending on the biological environment in which it develops. Likewise, at human conception one's substrate consciousness begins to emerge as a human mind and sense perceptions in dependence upon the gradual formation of a human brain and nervous system. The mind and various forms of sensory and mental consciousness do not emerge from the brain (as is widely assumed but never proven in modern science) but rather from the substrate consciousness. At death, these human mental functions do not simply disappear, as materialists believe (again without any compelling evidence), but rather dissolve back into the substrate consciousness, which carries on into the bardo and successive lives.

We normally configure consciousness with language, experience, personal identity, personal history, hopes and fears, joys and sorrows, and so on, but now we "experience a state of unstructured consciousness devoid of anything on which to meditate." There is no clear-cut object of meditation at this point. Once again, that's what makes it so easy to mistake this experience for either the realization of emptiness or rigpa. In Dzogchen texts "unmodified" usually refers to rigpa. But this is not rigpa. This is still at a grosser level.

"Then, when their awareness reaches the state of great nonmeditation, their guru points this out, so that they do not go astray." Now he is referring to deep Mahamudra and Dzogchen realization. The term *great nonmeditation* is very specific—you have reached ground awareness. Here you are definitely tapping into rigpa; and from that point on, as he said earlier, you simply take that ground awareness, rigpa, as the path.

"For this to occur, first you undergo great struggles in seeking the path; you take the movement of thoughts as the path; and finally, when consciousness settles upon itself, this is identified as the path. Until

> unstructured awareness, or consciousness, of the path manifests and
> rests in itself, because of the perturbations of your afflicted mind, you
> must gradually go through rough experiences like the ones discussed."

Once again the Bhagavan summarizes the path: "For this to occur, first you
undergo great struggles in seeking the path." That can be read in so many
ways. It could suggest that your having come to this teaching is an indica-
tion that you have an enormous amount of positive karma from your already
having progressed along other spiritual paths in past lives. You must have
struggled a lot in the past to find a path suited to you. No doubt you have
struggled greatly just to get to the point where you would even consider
achieving shamatha or think that it would be really worthwhile, let alone
acquiring the motivation to practice. Also, practice means sacrificing other
things, which no doubt is a struggle. On top of that are all those general
maladies that appear, such as back problems, disease, and so on.

First, "you undergo great struggles in seeking the path; you take the
movement of thoughts as the path"—the practice of shamatha—"and
finally, when consciousness settles upon itself, this is identified as the path."
At that point you take the mind as the path to enlightenment. "Until
unstructured awareness, or consciousness, of the path manifests and rests in
itself"—here he still seems to be speaking about shamatha. He uses
"unstructured" within the context of the mind and its ground. To "rest in
itself" here means until it settles in the substrate consciousness. Until then,
"because of the perturbations of your afflicted mind, you must gradually
go through rough experiences like the ones discussed." Why? Again, it's
because those problems are already there. You cannot bypass your mind to
get to enlightenment; you have to go through it. Nor can you bypass your
karma. You have to proceed from where you are, and there is no path to the
Great Perfection except by way of your own mind.

> Bodhisattva Great Boundless Emptiness then asked, "O Bhagavan,
> are thoughts to be cleared away or not? If they are, must con-
> sciousness emerge again after the mind has been purified? Teacher,
> please explain!"

The Teacher replied, "O Vajra of Mind, the rope of mindfulness and firmly maintained attention is dissolved by the power of meditative experiences, until finally the ordinary mind of an ordinary being disappears, as it were. Consequently, compulsive thinking subsides, and roving thoughts vanish into the space of awareness. You then slip into the vacuity of the substrate, in which self, others, and objects disappear. By clinging to the experiences of vacuity and clarity while looking inward, the appearances of self, others, and objects vanish. This is the substrate consciousness. Some teachers say that the substrate to which you descend is freedom from conceptual elaboration or the one taste, but others say it is ethically neutral. Whatever they call it, in truth you have come to the essential nature of the mind.

The ordinary mind is is cluttered with obsessive thoughts. Bodhisattva Great Boundless Emptiness wants to know if having cleared them out, does a new level of consciousness arise?

The Teacher replies that mindfulness and firmly maintained attention are "dissolved by the power of meditative experiences, until finally the ordinary mind of an ordinary being disappears, as it were." *Mindfulness*, remember, is the faculty of continuous sustained attention upon a familiar object. Here, "rope of mindfulness" suggests a subject over here and an object over there, held in place, tied down by mindfulness. However, when shamatha is achieved, the ordinary mind of the ordinary being disappears, as it were, into the substrate consciousness. Asanga, the great fifth-century Indian Buddhist contemplative scholar, also said that mindfulness is released after achieving shamatha.[29] You reach a point where the mindfulness that you were cultivating and sustaining previously becomes effortless and is released, leaving you simply present in the substrate consciousness. So you are no longer attending with mindfulness—you are no longer holding on to an object without forgetfulness. This happens by the power of meditative experiences, including all the nasty ones as well as the really beautiful ones. They serve to disentangle and break down the fabricated structure of your mind and bring it to the ground level.

Normally we spend a great deal of time being mentally afflicted, dominated by craving and hostility. Our home, our habitual resting place, is down in the swamp of afflictions. The accomplishment of shamatha reverses that. You will still be assaulted by mental afflictions once in a while, but you maintain yourself above that by sustaining a buoyant, supple state of consciousness that is highly resistant to being dominated by the imbalances of the mind. On the rare occasions when you slip below, you keep on springing back up. With shamatha it's so easy to go up and so hard to go down. For example, when your heart opens to loving-kindness, you may first bring to mind the dearest person in your whole life, and next the person who's been the most difficult for you, and there is just no difference between them. You no longer need to make greater effort to encompass your "worst enemy" within loving-kindness equal to that directed to your closest friend. That's when the classifications of "loved one," "friend," "neutral person," and "people I don't like" or "who don't like me"—those artificial demarcations of sentient beings—dissolve completely. The experience of loving-kindness becomes boundless—opens up immeasurably. That is spoken of as "achieving shamatha in loving-kindness."

Once you've done that, why not achieve such equilibrium all over again in compassion, and then in the rest of the four immeasurables—empathetic joy and equanimity? With shamatha as your platform it becomes feasible to break down all of these barriers completely. There are many contemplative scholars within Tibetan Buddhism who say it is not possible to achieve bodhichitta—to become a bodhisattva such that your bodhichitta is utterly effortless and rises spontaneously—without first accomplishing shamatha. You actually have to have shamatha in order to blossom as a bodhisattva, because if you don't have it, you have a dysfunctional mind. Due to old habits this dysfunctional mind is wobbling around between excitation and laxity, which is a poor basis for developing bodhichitta—something that's going to be with you from now until enlightenment. So the sublime sanity of shamatha is the basis for vipashyana, for bodhichitta, for the stages of generation and completion, and for Dzogchen.

The meditative experiences, then, are enabling the ordinary mind of an ordinary being to disappear—to unravel and dissolve back into the sub-

strate consciousness. "Consequently, compulsive thinking subsides, and roving thoughts vanish into the space of awareness." Here "space of awareness" refers to the space of the mind, the substrate. Notice he's not saying
that you have to clear them away volitionally. He tells us that this happens
naturally, effortlessly.

"You then slip into the vacuity of the substrate, in which self, others, and
objects disappear." I've chosen the word *vacuity* rather than *emptiness* because
this shouldn't be mistaken for the realization that all phenomena lack inherent nature. It's just empty, vacuous. There is nothing in it. The substrate is
the *alaya;* substrate consciousness is the *alayavijñana.* When you slip into the
substrate consciousness, what you're attending to, experiencing, what's
appearing to your mind, to your substrate consciousness, is the substrate,
the *alaya.* The *alaya* is a vacuity in which self, others, and objects disappear.
There are no appearances except for an occasional "bubble." The substrate,
the *alaya,* is luminous, but empty.

"Space of awareness," as we've seen, is the translation for the Sanskrit
word *dhatu.* In this context, the space of awareness, or *dhatu,* is none other
than the substrate. That's the sheer vacuity to which you are attending;
that's the space of the mind that is empty. *Dhatu* is certainly a tricky term,
having different meanings in different contexts. For example, *dhatu* is often
a contraction of *dharmadhatu,* which I translate as the "absolute space of phenomena." In the context of Dzogchen, *dharmadhatu* refers to the ultimate
ground—the ground of all of samsara and nirvana, which is nondual from
primordial consciousness. If there are multiple possible universes, plus nirvana, conventional reality, ultimate reality, the whole shebang—rigpa is
the ground of the whole, which is nondual from the absolute space of phenomena, *dharmadhatu.* It is not just the ground *from which* the whole arises. It's
the ground that is the one taste of them all, of samsara and nirvana.

That is definitely not true of the substrate. The substrate is not the
ground of nirvana. It is the ground of samsara, your own particular samsara. You can get to that space by withdrawing from the senses and from
conceptualization—by simplifying and going into the cubbyhole of your
substrate. Although that is not rigpa, Düdjom Lingpa says this experience of bliss, luminosity, and vacuity is indispensable on the path. We can

postpone the achievement of shamatha as long as we like, while venturing into far more esoteric meditations. But if we want to come to the culmination of the cultivation of bodhichitta, vipashyana, the stages of generation and completion, and Dzogchen, sooner or later we need to focus single-pointedly on shamatha practice and carry through with it until our minds dissolve into the substrate consciousness as Düdjom Lingpa describes. This may take months or even years of full-time shamatha practice, and that calls for real sacrifice. But if we refuse to take up this challenge, all the other more advanced practices we explore are bound to hit a ceiling that we cannot transcend due to the imbalances of excitation and laxity that we have yet to overcome.

How does all of this relate to the *Vajra Essence*, to the place we have now reached within this particular text? In this context, when you've achieved shamatha, roving thoughts have all dissolved. Your mind, as it were, dissolves, your mind being the ordinary mind of an ordinary human being. That's all dissolved into the substrate consciousness; this dimension of consciousness that is the luminous, vacuous ground of the ordinary mind.

"By clinging to the experiences of vacuity and clarity...": Vacuity can still be regarded as a sign or as an object. If you can cling to it, it's a sign, so this is still relative mind. Remember that these experiences are nyam and that we get nyam all the way up to the realization of rigpa. "By clinging to the experiences of vacuity and clarity while looking inward, the appearances of self, others, and objects vanish." The whole notion of looking inward, withdrawing from the world of the senses, withdrawing from conceptualization, the senses shutting down—all of this is characteristic of shamatha and not of authentic Dzogchen practice. So, you slip into the vacuity of the substrate consciousness, in which the appearances of "self, others, and objects vanish." This is exactly what Asanga says, so there is secondary confirmation here.[30] You are experiencing the substrate consciousness, also known as the continuum of subtle mental consciousness. That is what your coarse mind has been reduced to. The ground of your ordinary mind is the substrate consciousness. Now what is the substrate consciousness attending to? What is appearing to it? It's the substrate—that vacuity, an emptiness. What makes it luminous? Your own consciousness, which is empty and yet luminous, but it is not luminous by its own nature independent of rigpa. Ultimately, as we saw previously, it is illuminated by primordial consciousness.

"Some teachers say the substrate to which you descend"—note the word, "descend," you are settling into it—"is freedom from conceptual elaboration or the one taste." *Freedom from conceptual elaboration* is one of the stages of the four yogas of Mahamudra,[31] a very deep, profound realization of primordial consciousness. So some people arrive at the substrate and then give it this lofty title that is applied to an advanced stage of Mahamudra. *One taste* is another, even deeper level of Mahamudra yoga.

What he is saying, very clearly, is that some teachers mistake the substrate for the Mahamudra states of realization known as *freedom from conceptual elaboration* and the *one taste*, while "others say it is ethically neutral." This latter characterization is correct. This state is indeed ethically neutral. To dwell there is not profoundly transformative, certainly not in any irreversible way; and by dwelling there you do not accrue merit. You are treading water, hanging out in neutral. "Whatever they call it, in truth you have come to the essential nature of the mind." You have come to the culmination of this practice, and you realize the nature of the mind, the *conventional* nature of the mind, the *relative* nature of the mind. When he speaks of "essential nature" he is not referring to the emptiness of inherent nature of the mind or to rigpa. He is referring to unadorned consciousness as it is present prior to being configured by biological and environmental influences. Here is consciousness stripped bare, down to its essential nature of luminosity and cognizance. So now you know what the mind is in a pretty deep sense, because this is not just your psyche. It is the ground from which your psyche emerges.

DEEPER POSSIBILITIES OF SHAMATHA PRACTICE

> "On the other hand, someone with enthusiastic perseverance may recognize that this is not the authentic path, and by continuing to meditate, all such experiences tainted by clinging to a blankness, vacuity, and luminosity vanish into the space of awareness, as if you

were waking up. Subsequently, outer appearances are not impeded, and the rope of inner mindfulness and firmly maintained attention is cut. Then you are not bound by the constraints of good meditation, nor do you fall back to an ordinary state through pernicious ignorance. Rather, ever-present, translucent, luminous consciousness shines through, transcending the conventions of view, meditation, and conduct. Without dichotomizing self and object, such that you can say 'this is consciousness' and 'this is the object of consciousness,' the primordial, self-originating mind is freed from clinging to experiences.

A student "with enthusiastic perseverance may recognize that this is not the authentic path"—may even realize this at an early stage. This is not the direct means for realizing rigpa. "By continuing to meditate, all such experiences tainted by clinging to a blankness, vacuity, and luminosity vanish into the space of awareness, as if you were waking up." He is showing that this practice has higher possibilities. If you enter this practice with intelligence and zeal, recognize the limitations of slipping into the substrate consciousness, and see the problems of clinging to any of its signs—clinging to the experiences of bliss, luminosity, and nonconceptuality—those experiences "vanish into the space of awareness." So even these three distinct qualities of the substrate vanish, "as if you were waking up."

Bear in mind that the substrate consciousness is the dimension of awareness we enter when we fall into deep, dreamless sleep. Now you awaken from that luminous deep sleep, awaken from the substrate consciousness. "Subsequently, outer appearances are not impeded," as they were in the substrate, "and the rope of inner mindfulness and firmly maintained attention is cut." So there is no rope attaching you either to the substrate or to any sign, and no firmly maintained attention, no effortful striving with diligence. That rope is cut.

"Then you are not bound by the constraints of good meditation, nor do you fall back to an ordinary state through pernicious ignorance. Rather, ever-present, translucent, luminous consciousness shines through, transcending the conventions of view, meditation, and conduct. Without dichotomizing self and object, such that you can say 'this is consciousness' and 'this is the object of consciousness,' the primordial, self-originating mind is freed from clinging to experiences." It is here that we transcend shamatha and the substrate consciousness, breaking through to pristine awareness. Notice how smoothly and how simply it can happen.

> "When you settle into a spaciousness in which there is no cogitation or referent of the attention, all phenomena become manifest, for the power of awareness is unimpeded. Thoughts merge with their objects, disappearing as they become nondual with those objects, and they dissolve. Since not a single one has an objective referent, they are not thoughts of sentient beings; instead, the mind is transformed into wisdom, the power of awareness is transformed, and stability is achieved there. Understand this to be like water that is clear of sediment."

"When you settle into a spaciousness in which there is no cogitation or referent of the attention"—no signs, that is, you are no longer withdrawn into the substrate consciousness—"all phenomena become manifest, for the power of awareness is unimpeded." To be withdrawn from all appearances and simply dwell in a blank vacuity is relatively easy. You can even imagine it. To be grasping on to signs and reifying them, we are certainly familiar with that. Rigpa, however, is inconceivable and ineffable. Düdjom Lingpa is speaking here about there being no referent of attention, and yet all phenomena continue to manifest. "The power of awareness is unimpeded." Awareness is not withdrawn into itself. It is free. "Thoughts merge with their objects"—here I think he is stretching language as far as it can go without snapping—"disappearing as they become nondual with those objects, and they dissolve. Since not a single one"—of those thoughts—"has an objective referent, they are not thoughts of sentient beings; instead, the mind is transformed into wisdom, the power of awareness is transformed, and stability is achieved there. Understand this to be like water that is clear of sediment."

* * *

In this opening section of the *Vajra Essence*, Düdjom Lingpa reveals the nature of the mind and then shows us how to take our own minds, with all their afflictions and obscurations, as our path to realizing the relative ground state of awareness, the substrate consciousness. And once the mind has dissolved into this blissful, luminous vacuity, he shows us how to break through our individuated mindstreams and realize our true nature—pristine awareness that has never been tainted by any obscurations. He has made this path clear, accessible, and inviting. Without the achievement of shamatha, none of our meditations will bring about irreversible transformation and liberation. But once we have settled our minds in their natural state, the entire path to the Great Perfection lies before us, beckoning for us to realize our true nature in this very lifetime. There can be no greater adventure, no greater frontier to explore, and no greater freedom to realize than this Great Perfection, the one taste of samsara and nirvana.

NOTES

1 The full title is *The Vajra Essence: From the Matrix of Pure Appearances and Primordial Consciousness, a Tantra on the Self-Originating Nature of Existence* (*Dag snang ye shes drva pa las gnas lugs rang byung gi rgyud rdo rje'i snying po*; Sanskrit title: *Vajrahṛdayasuddhadbhuti-jñānahāresrīlamjātiyātisma*).

2 A *terma*, or "treasure," is a hidden text or object, which may be hidden in the ground, water, space, or even mindstream of an adept, waiting to be discovered by a "treasure-revealer" (*tertön*) when the time is most propitious.

3 The form realm, formless realm, and desire realm. Humans and the other five types of existence are in the desire realm. The highest heaven realms make up the form realm. Noncorporeal gods in meditative absorption comprise the formless realm.

4 *Lamp for the Path to Enlightenment*, verse 35.

5 The *dhyanas* are advanced states of meditative concentration.

6 See Marvin Minsky, *The Society of Mind* (New York: Simon & Schuster, 1986).

7 *A Guide to the Bodhisattva Way of Life* 10:55.

8 Suffice it to say that a "countless eon" is an immensely long, but still finite, period of time.

9 *A Guide to the Bodhisattva Way of Life* 1:21.

10 *Samadhi*, in the narrow sense of the term, means focused concentration, but in the broader sense implied within this triad, it refers to exceptional states of mental balance and well-being.

11 According to the philosopher Martin Buber, an "I-it" relationship dehumanizes the person who is viewed as an "it." An "I-you" relationship acknowledges the subjective reality of the other person as a "you," and an "I-thou" relationship transcends the polarized distinction of self and other, embracing both in a large, encompassing entirety.

12 *Dhammapada* 3:33–34.

13 *A Guide to the Bodhisattva Way of Life* 1:14.

14 *A Guide to the Bodhisattva Way of Life* 1:18.

15   *Dhammapada* 1:1.

16   Ven. Weragoda Sarada Maha Thero, *Treasury of Truth: Illustrated Dhammapada* (Taipei, Taiwan: The Corporate Body of the Buddha Education Foundation, 1993), p. 61.

17   Stephen W. Hawking and Thomas Hertog, "Populating the Landscape: A Top-Down Approach," *Physical Review D* 73.123527 (2006); Martin Bojowald, "Unique or Not Unique?" *Nature* 442 (Aug. 31, 2006): 988–90.

18   Bruce Greyson, "Implications of Near-Death Experiences for a Postmaterialist Psychology," *Psychology of Religion and Spirituality* 2.1 (2010): 37–45; Ian Stevenson, *Where Reincarnation and Biology Intersect* (New York: Praeger, 1997).

19   Francisco J. Varela, ed., *Sleeping, Dreaming, and Dying: An Exploration of Consciousness with the Dalai Lama*, trans. by Thupten Jinpa and B. Alan Wallace (Boston: Wisdom Publications, 1997), pp. 204–13.

20   *Ratnameghasūtra*, cited in Sāntideva, *Sikṣāsamuccaya*, trans. by Cecil Bendall and W. H. D. Rouse (Delhi: Motilal Banarsidass, 1981), p. 121.

21   William James, *The Principles of Psychology*, 2 vols. (New York: Dover Publications, 1950), vol. 2, p. 322.

22   Padmasambhava, *Natural Liberation: Padmasambhava's Teachings on the Six Bardos*, commentary by Gyatrul Rinpoche, trans. B. Alan Wallace (Boston: Wisdom Publications, 2008), pp. 105–16.

23   Jiddu Krishnamurti and David Bohm, *The Ending of Time* (Madras: Krishnamurti Foundation India, 1992), p. 85.

24   Düdjom Lingpa and Düdjom Rinpoche, *The Vajra Quintessence: A Compilation of Three Texts on the Great Perfection*, with annotations by the Venerable Gyatrul Rinpoche, trans. B. Alan Wallace and Chandra Easton (Ashland, OR: Vimala Publishing, 2011), p. 46.

25   *Kevaddha Sutta*, DN I 223; cf. Maurice Walshe, *The Long Discourses of the Buddha: A Translation of the Dīgha Nikāya* (Boston: Wisdom Publications, 1995), pp. 179–80.

26   Padmasambhava, *Natural Liberation*, p. 114 (with minor modifications).

27   For more description of the five elements as they pertain to individuals, see Tenzin Wangyal Rinpoche's *Healing with Form, Energy, and Light* (Ithaca, NY: Snow Lion Publications, 2002).

28   *Udāna* 8:3.

29   Cf. B. Alan Wallace, *Balancing the Mind: A Tibetan Buddhist Approach to Refining Attention* (Ithaca, NY: Snow Lion Publications, 2005), p. 205.

30   Cf. Wallace, *Balancing the Mind*, p. 206.

31   The four stages, or yogas of Mahamudra, which culminate in buddhahood, are: (1) single-pointed samadhi, where you first gain access—the union of shamatha and vipashyana; (2) the freedom from conceptual elaboration; (3) the one taste; and (4) no meditation.

GLOSSARY

afflictions/mental afflictions (Skt. *klesha*). Aversion, craving, delusion, and so forth; mental disturbances that propel us to perform negative actions and perpetuate samsara.

alaya (Skt). *See* substrate

alayavijñana (Skt). *See* substrate consciousness

arhat (Skt). One who has achieved nirvana, the complete cessation of the causes of suffering and their effects.

arya (Skt). One who has gained a nonconceptual, unmediated realization of emptiness on the path of seeing.

awareness (Skt. *vidya*). Usually rigpa in this book, but sometimes consciousness more generally.

bardo (Tib. *bar do*). The intermediate state between one life and the next.

bindu (Skt). In the present book, a tiny visualized luminous sphere the size of pea or smaller.

bodhichitta (Skt). *Relative bodhichitta* is the heartfelt wish to achieve enlightenment for the benefit of all beings. *Ultimate bodhichitta* in general Mahayana Buddhism is the realization of emptiness, whereas in Dzogchen it is rigpa.

buddha nature (Skt. *tathagatagarbha*). In the context of Dzogchen, this is a synonym for dharmakaya, or primordial consciousness, and it is the mind's ultimate nature.

buddhafield. A pure land that was created through the positive aspiration of a buddha while still a bodhisattva; synonymous with "pure land."

chö (Tib. *gcod*). A yoga for severing self-grasping and the name of a Tibetan teaching lineage centered on this yoga.

clarity. *See* luminosity

clear light. *See* luminosity

completion stage. *See* stage of completion

conceptual elaboration (Skt. *prapancha*). The proliferation of conceptualization.

conventional reality (Skt. *samvritisatya*). The world of appearances, as opposed to ultimate reality, which is the emptiness of those appearances.

dakini (Skt). Female enlightened being who comes to the aid of tantric yogis.

delusion (Skt. *avidya*). The mental affliction that projects inherent existence onto phenomena; the root affliction that produces all the others and is the root cause of samsara.

desire realm (Skt. *kamadhatu*). The level of existence that includes hell beings, hungry ghosts, animals, humans, demigods, and the lesser gods.

dharmadhatu (Skt). Absolute space of phenomena.

dharmakaya (Skt). The "truth body"; reality for a buddha, which is the ultimate reality. Synonymous with the buddha mind and buddha nature.

dharmata (Skt). *See* ultimate reality

dhyana (Skt; Pali *jhana*). Advanced states of meditative concentration, generally presented in four progressively deeper levels.

divine pride. The Vajrayana practice of first recognizing the conventional nature of your own, ordinary identity and then replacing it with a sense of yourself as being identical to a buddha.

dream yoga. Performing Dharma practice in one's sleep through lucid dreaming.

Dzogchen (Tib. *rdzogs chen*). The pinnacle yoga of Tibetan Buddhism, especially for the Nyingma school, where one rests in the primordial consciousness.

emptiness (Skt. *shunyata*). The absence of inherent existence of all phenomena.

equipoise. *See* meditative equipoise

excitation (Skt. *auddhatya*). Mental hyperactivity that prevents focus. One of the two imbalances to which the mind is habitually prone and that are overcome through the practice of shamatha.

form realm (Skt. *rupadhatu*). Samsaric level of existence that includes the extremely long-lived gods of Akanishta and is characterized by abiding in blissful absorption.

formless realm (Skt. *arupadhatu*). The pinnacle of samsaric existence, where beings have no material form and abide in single-pointed meditation.

four applications of mindfulness. A standard set of objects for mindfulness meditation: mindfulness of the body, feelings, mental states, and mental objects.

four immeasurables. Loving-kindness, compassion, empathetic joy, and equanimity.

four thoughts that turn the mind (Tib. *blo ldog rnam bzhi*). Meditations on the preciousness and rarity of fully endowed human life, on impermanence and death, on the reality of suffering, and on the nature of karma.

Gelug. One of the four major Tibetan Buddhist schools, with a distinctive emphasis on monasticism and rigorous scholastic training.

generation stage. *See* stage of generation

Great Perfection. *See* Dzogchen

ground awareness (Tib. *gzhi' rig pa*). A synonym for primordial consciousness. *See* rigpa

inherent existence (Skt. *svabhavasiddhi*). A quality projected onto phenomena by the deluded mind. An inherent existence is a self-sufficient essence that things appear to possess that makes them seem to exist independently from the mind conceiving of them.

insight. Most often refers to vipashyana, but can refer to the realization of other phenomena besides emptiness, too.

introspection (Skt. *samprajanya*). The faculty of monitoring the quality of one's body, speech, and mind. In the practice of shamatha this pertains especially to monitoring the flow of attention, being on guard for the occurrence of laxity and excitation.

Jigmé Lingpa (1729–98). A famous terma discoverer and a highly influential Nyingma master.

jñana (Skt). Literally "knowledge," but often refers to primordial consciousness.

Kagyü. One of the four major Tibetan Buddhist schools, with a distinctive emphasis on Mahamudra meditation and the six Dharmas of Naropa.

Karma Chagmé Rinpoche (1613–78). A master who combined the meditation teachings of the Nyingma and Kagyü traditions.

karmic imprint (Skt. *vasana*). The seed planted in the substrate consciousness by one's past actions and intentions that will ripen as an experience upon meeting suitable conditions. *See also* propensities

klesha. *See* afflictions/mental afflictions

laxity (Skt. *laya*). One of the two imbalances to which the mind is habitually prone; is counteracted through the cultivation of vividness in the practice of shamatha.

luminosity (Skt. *prabhasvara*). The natural clarity of awareness that makes manifest all appearances.

Madhyamaka. A philosophical school originating in India in the second century with Nagarjuna that became the dominant strain of Tibetan Buddhist philosophy. Stresses the emptiness of all phenomena and the freedom from the extremes of nihilism and realism, thus its name, the "Middle Way."

Mahamudra (Skt). Meditation on the ultimate nature of the mind that is particularly prominent in the Kagyü school.

mara (Skt). A mental affliction, often personified as an external being.

meditative equipoise (Skt. *samahita*). A meditative state characterized by deep stillness and clarity.

meditative quiescence. *See* shamatha

mental affliction. *See* afflictions/mental afflictions

merit (Skt. *punya*). Karmic potential generated through performing positive actions with a virtuous motivation.

Milarepa (1040–1123). Famous yogi of the eleventh century known for his ascetic feats and his songs of realization.

mindfulness (Skt. *smriti*; Pali *sati*). The faculty of continuous sustained attention upon a familiar object.

Mipham Rinpoche (1846–1912). Important Nyingma master of the nineteenth century who was strongly affiliated with the ecumenical (*rime*) movement and whose scholastic works became central for the Nyingma monastic curriculum.

nimitta (Skt). An archetypal form or sign that appears to the meditator to indicate passage through a particular phase.

nirmanakaya (Skt). The body of a buddha visible to ordinary beings that manifests to guide those with sufficient merit along the path.

Nyingma. Oldest of the four major schools of Tibetan Buddhism.

one taste. The third of four yogas of the Mahamudra tradition wherein whatever is experienced is known to be the mind.

Padmasambhava. Eighth-century Bengali tantric master who helped usher Buddhism into Tibet and is revered as a second Buddha in the eyes of many Tibetan Buddhists.

paths. Buddhism speaks of five progressive levels of realization on the way to buddhahood: the paths of accumulation, preparation, seeing, meditation, and no more training.

phowa (Tib. *'pho ba*). *See* transference of consciousness

pliancy (Skt. *prasrabdhi*). The suppleness and buoyancy of the mind that is cultivated through the practice of shamatha.

pointing-out instructions. When a teacher conveys the nature of the mind, or rigpa, to a student.

post-meditation. The period between formal sessions of meditation.

prana (Skt). The vital energies that course through the body, closely related to the central nervous system.

pratyekabuddha (Skt). A "solitary realizer": Hinayana practitioner who strives to realize nirvana and become an arhat without the benefit of a teacher in the present life.

primordial consciousness (Skt. *jñana*). *See* rigpa

primordial ground (Tib. *gdod ma'i gzhi*). The absolute space of phenomena, nondual from primordial consciousness.

pristine awareness (Skt. *vidya*). Synonym for primordial consciousness. *See* rigpa

propensities (Skt. *vasana*). Karmically conditioned tendencies or habits; the seeds of past actions stored in the substrate consciousness that will ripen as future experiences.

pure vision. The tantric practice of viewing all beings and phenomena as manifestations of the Buddha.

quiescence. *See* shamatha

realization (Tib. *rtogs pa*). Direct insight into fundamental features of reality that liberates that mind from afflictions and obscurations.

reification (Tib. *bden 'dzin*). Grasping on to inherent existence; projecting true existence onto empty phenomena.

rigpa (Skt. *vidya*). Pristine awareness, the absolute ground state of consciousness, more profound than the substrate consciousness, for it pervades all of reality and not just one's own mind.

samadhi (Skt). In the narrow sense of the term, means focused concentration (achieved through the practice of shamatha), but in the broader sense it is one of the three "higher trainings," together with ethics and wisdom. In that context it refers to exceptional states of mental balance and well-being.

sambhogakaya (Skt). A buddha's "enjoyment body," a rarefied form, perceptible only to highly realized beings, that is complete with the marks and signs and is adorned with elaborate jewels and elegant apparel.

samsara (Skt). Cyclic existence; a being's circling among the six realms through the force of karma and mental afflictions.

secret mantra. Tantra.

self-originating (Tib. *rang 'byung*). Arising spontaneously from the absolute space of phenomena.

settling the mind in its natural state (Tib. *sems rnal du babs pa*). Allowing the coarse mind to dissolve into its underlying continuum of subtle consciousness known in the Dzogchen tradition as the substrate consciousness.

shamatha (Skt). Meditative practices designed to refine the attention and balance the mind in preparation for the practice of vipashyana.

shravaka (Skt). A Buddhist practitioner who is set on achieving individual liberation, based on listening to and following the Buddha's teachings.

siddhis (Skt). Capacities we obtain as we advance in meditation. These include supernormal powers such as clairvoyance, walking on water, flying, and a number of other abilities.

six realms of existence. The abodes of hell beings, hungry ghosts, animals, humans, demigods, and gods.

six perfections. The quintessential bodhisattva endeavors, the perfection of generosity, ethics, patience, enthusiasm, meditation, and wisdom.

skillful means (Skt. *upaya*). A buddha's capacity to tailor instructions to the particular mindset of each individual. Can also just mean the method by which one advances along the path.

space of awareness (Skt. *dhatu*). *See* substrate

stage of completion. The second of the two main stages of tantra, wherein one manipulates the energies of the subtle body to produce samadhi on ultimate reality.

stage of generation. The first of the two main stages of tantra, wherein one builds up the visualization of the deity and the mandala, makes offerings, and practices pure vision.

substrate (Skt. *alaya*). The space of the mind that appears to the substrate consciousness: a luminous vacuity in which self, others, and objects disappear.

substrate consciousness (Skt. *alayavijñana*). The ground of the ordinary mind, a continuum that travels from life to life and from which springs all ordinary mental activity.

terma (Tib. *gter ma*). A "treasure," or hidden text or object, which may be hidden in the ground, water, space, or even mindstream of an adept, waiting to be discovered by a "treasure-revealer" (*tertön*) when the time is most propitious.

three realms. The desire, form, and formless realms; samsaric existence.

tögal (Tib. *thod rgal*). "Direct crossing-over," the second of two stages of Dzogchen in which the dynamic potentials of primordial consciousness are made fully manifest, resulting in the achievement of buddhahood.

tonglen (Tib. *gtong len*). The meditative practice of "sending and taking," where you imagine sending all your virtue and happiness to other sentient beings, while taking upon yourself all the nonvirtue and misery of the world.

transference of consciousness (Skt. *samkranti*; Tib. *'pho ba*). A yoga for ejecting the consciousness at the time of death into a pure realm body.

treasury of space (Tib. *nam mkha'i mdzod*). Interchangeable with ultimate reality.

tregchö (Tib. *khregs chod*). "Breakthrough," the first of two stages of Dzogchen, designed to break through the substrate consciousness to a direct realization of pristine awareness, which is synonymous with one's own buddha nature.

true existence (Skt. *satyasat*). Same as inherent existence.

Tsongkhapa (1357–1419). Founder of the Gelug school, teacher of the First Dalai Lama, and one of the greatest scholars and contemplatives of Tibet.

tulku (Tib. *sprul sku*). The Tibetan word for *nirmanakaya*, often used to refer to those, typically lamas, who are formally recognized as incarnations of enlightened beings.

tummo (Tib. *gtum mo;* Skt. *chandali*). A yoga for generating of states of bliss and insight through generating heat in the navel chakra, causing subtle essences at the crown to melt and descend through the chakras below.

ultimate reality (Skt. *dharmata*). The ultimate mode of being of all dharmas, i.e., emptiness.

vacuity (Tib. *stong pa*). An absence. This is "an emptiness" as opposed to "emptiness qua the ultimate reality of all phenomena."

vajra (Skt). Diamond-like, immutable. Often used as shorthand for Vajrayana, or tantra.

Vajradhara. The form of the Buddha when he imparted the tantras.

vidyadhara (Skt). One who has gained a conceptually unmediated, nondual realization of rigpa, of buddha nature.

vipashyana (Skt). Contemplative insight into fundamental aspects of reality, including the emptiness of inherent nature of all phenomena.

vital energy. *See* prana

wisdom (Skt. *prajña*). The sixth of the six perfections that characterize the bodhisattva way of life, and the culminating phase of the three higher trainings in ethics, samadhi, and wisdom.

Yogachara. One of two dominant philosophical schools of Mahayana Buddhism originating in India, along with the Madhyamaka school. Also called the Mind Only (Chittamatra) school, as it teaches that that external phenomena have no reality apart from the mind apprehending them.

INDEX

four thoughts that turn the mind and,
64
karma and, 69
mindfulness of, 42, 45–46
separation of matter and awareness at,
68, 69, 71, 80
delusion, 71, 94–95, 103, 116–17, 169
afflictive cognition and, 22
described, 184
Devadatta and, 17
demons, 128–29, 132, 142, 160, 162
depression, xii, 48, 114, 124, 164, 166
Descartes, René, 92
desire realm, 106, 127, 153, 184
Devadatta, 17
dharmadhatu, 2, 31, 184. See also space
dharmakaya, xii, 7, 11, 13–14, 32–33,
49, 72–73, 102, 105, 159
accomplishing shamatha and, 154
described, 184
grasping and, 8
ordinary mind and, 22
dharmata, 3, 63, 184. See also emptiness;
ultimate reality
dhyanas, 17, 154, 184
direct crossing-over. See tögal
dismemberment, sensations of, 142
divine pride, 8, 9, 16, 28, 72, 122, 184
dream(s), 36, 69, 88, 90–91, 94, 117
body, 81, 82, 86
lucid, 17, 81
yoga, 65, 184
dualism, 2, 6, 14, 106, 133
Düdjom Lingpa, vii–xiv, 4–21, 35–36,
49, 116, 119, 158, 165–66
cosmological descriptions and, 78
inner preliminaries and, 64
on meditative stabilization, 121, 133
on the path, 175–76
on the power of awareness, 179
Dungi Zurphu, xiv

Dzogchen, xiii, 1–2, 39–42, 50–65, 83,
97, 102–3, 105
achieving stability and, 121
enlightenment and, 157
grasping and, 9
introduction to, ix, 184
nonmeditation and, 171
open presence and, 133
samsara and, 169
shamatha and, 154–55, 174
Dzogpa, use of the term, 39–40

E
eating habits, 131
ego, 11, 15, 27. See also self
electromagnetic fields, 71, 91–93,
128–29
emptiness, 8, 21, 39, 43, 184
and bodhichitta, 57–58, 65
distinct from substrate, 171, 175, 176
in Dzogchen, ix, 58, 154
in five paths, 36, 37
and knowledge, 102–3
and provisional truths, 78
realization of, 3, 13, 30, 36, 58, 102–3,
105, 153, 171
and shamatha, xi, 63, 142, 177
as ultimate reality, 3, 63, 88, 104, 105
unoriginated, 84–85
empty vessel, metaphor of, 4
enlightenment, xii, xiii, 28–30, 36, 44,
50–53, 58–59, 131, 156, 172
achievement of, 28, 29, 33, 78, 120–21
"letting thoughts be as they are" and,
116
primordial consciousness and, 32
samsara and, 71, 103
shamatha and, 105, 114
stage of generation and, 72
symbols of, 19
equanimity, 57, 167, 175

buddha nature and, 63
described, 132, 190
Devadatta and, 17
shamatha and, 39, 50–51, 62, 122, 125
vipassana practice, 132–33

W
water
"excellent," eight qualities of, 18
metaphor using, 3, 10, 12
wind disorders, 114
wisdom, 13, 37, 38, 39, 43, 44, 65, 190.
See also prajña

wish-fulfilling jewel, metaphor of, 50
womb, metaphor of, 11–12, 25–26
Words of My Perfect Teacher (Patrül Rinpoche), vii
working hypothesis, 43, 44, 54

Y
yidam, 5
yoga, 81, 82, 110, 177
Yogachara, xiii, 190

Z
Zen Buddhism, 121, 169

ABOUT THE AUTHOR

B. Alan Wallace is president of the Santa Barbara Institute for Consciousness Studies. He trained for many years as a monk in Buddhist monasteries in India and Switzerland. He has taught Buddhist theory and practice in Europe and America since 1976 and has served as interpreter for numerous Tibetan scholars and contemplatives, including H. H. the Dalai Lama.

After graduating *summa cum laude* from Amherst College, where he studied physics and the philosophy of science, he earned his MA and PhD in religious studies at Stanford University. He has edited, translated, authored, and contributed to more than forty books on Tibetan Buddhism, medicine, language, and culture, and the interface between science and religion.

After teaching for four years in the Department of Religious Studies at the University of California, Santa Barbara, he founded and currently serves as president of the Santa Barbara Institute for Consciousness Studies, which focuses on the interface between contemplative and scientific ways of exploring the mind and its potentials.

About Wisdom Publications

Wisdom Publications is the leading publisher of classic and contemporary Buddhist books and practical works on mindfulness. To learn more about us or to explore our other books, please visit our website at wisdompubs.org or contact us at the address below.

Wisdom Publications
199 Elm Street
Somerville, MA 02144 USA

We are a 501(c)(3) organization, and donations in support of our mission are tax deductible.

Wisdom Publications is affiliated with the Foundation for the Preservation of the Mahayana Tradition (FPMT).